Fylde Coast and Country Walks

Fylde Coast and Country Walks

David Packer

First published in 2003
by Carnegie Publishing Ltd
Carnegie House, Chatsworth Road
Lancaster LA1 4SL

www.carnegiepublishing.com

Copyright © David Packer, 2003

All rights reserved

British Library Cataloguing-in-Publication data
A CIP record for this book is available from the British Library

ISBN 1-874181-20-9

Designed and typeset by Carnegie Publishing
Printed and bound in the UK by Cromwell Press, Trowbridge (Wilts)

Contents

Acknowledgements		vii
Introduction		1
Farming Year		4
Walk 1	Fleetwood	5
Walk 2	Thornton	10
Walk 3	Cleveleys and Thornton	15
Walk 4	North of Blackpool	21
Walk 5	Poulton-le-Fylde	25
Walk 6	Marton and Blackpool	28
Walk 7	Singleton	34
Walk 8	Weeton and Greenhalgh	39
Walk 9	Lytham	43
Walk 10	Around Wrea Green	47
Walk 11	Around Warton	51
Walk 12	Freckleton	54
Walk 13	From Kirkham	58
Walk 14	Salwick and Treales	62
Walk 15	South of Preston	67
Walk 16	From Woodplumpton	73
Walk 17	Around Inskip	76
Walk 18	Churchtown	79
Walk 19	Great and Little Eccleston	84
Walk 20	Pilling and Eagland Hill	88
Walk 21	Stalmine	94

Walk 22 Knott End-on-Sea	98
Walk 23 Pilling Marsh	102
Walk 24 Brock Valley and Bleasdale	106
Walk 25 Whitechapel and Beacon Fell	112
Walk 26 Inglewhite	116

Acknowledgements

I would like to acknowledge the assistance of the following organizations and individuals who either helped to resolve queries or checked some of the walks: Lancashire County Council Rights of Way Department at Preston, the National Farmers Union, the libraries at Fleetwood, St Annes and Lytham, Pilling and District Historical Society, John Higginson, John and Linda Adams, Glenice Webb, Carolyn Schofield and Eric, Joyce and Helen Packer.

Introduction

It doesn't matter where I travel nor how highly I rate the beauty spots of Britain, or the world for that matter, I still enjoy returning home; I am comforted by the sights of familiar features. Driving home north along the M6 motorway I look out for my first view of the Lancashire fells and then, heading west along the M55 motorway, I, subconsciously perhaps, look out for features such as the Lancaster Canal, Blackpool Tower and the windmill at Marton that help draw me closer to home. I believe that whichever area we live in most of us hold some feeling of affection for our home ground and admire qualities that may not be so apparent to the occasional visitor. Well, whether or not that theory is correct, I hope that the affection I feel for this area is somehow transmitted to the reader.

Although this book is entitled *Fylde Coast and Country Walks* the land covered stretches beyond the true borders of the Fylde. While the political area under the control of Fylde Borough Council includes Lytham St Annes, Kirkham, Freckleton and smaller villages, the geographical boundaries have been variously described as extending between the Ribble and the Wyre and the Ribble and the Lune. The latter description was admittedly given as a 'loose' boundary but, nevertheless, it is this extended version of the Fylde I intend to adopt. To be more precise the boundaries I have used extend from the Ribble in the south to the Lune estuary in the north and between the natural barriers of the coast in the west and the Lancashire fells in the east. The reason for my definition is because, to those living in the true area of the Fylde, this extended region will naturally be regarded as 'home' territory for the purposes of day trips and half-days out. It could be argued that there is also a spiritual bond with the fells to the east from whose slopes come the waters that add to the productivity of the land on the Fylde.

There are many features within the boundaries I have chosen that occur regularly in the walks – the hills, Parlick in particular, the main transport routes such as the M6, M55 and A6, the West Coast Main Line between London and Glasgow together with its branches to the Fylde coast, the rivers Ribble and Wyre and tributaries such as the Brock and Calder, and the Lancaster Canal – transport links of different eras. Then there are the man-made structures such as Blackpool Tower, the communications station at Inskip, the churches and, of course, the windmills, four with sails but most of them without. Finally, there is the land, gently rolling in parts and flat in other areas giving way to crops and vegetables, pastures, moorland, mosses, mudflats and beach. Already it can be seen that there is a remarkable variety of landscape and features for such a small geographical area and now, having done what I can to convince you of the merits of walking in this region of contrasts, all that remains is for me to ask you to try for yourself. If you are prepared to be convinced then please read the following notes of caution as it could save you and, indeed, others a lot of anguish, especially if you are not regular walkers:

1. In most instances the rights of way cross over private property, usually

Fylde Coast and Country Walks

belonging to farmers. It is very important to treat their land with respect thereby encouraging trusting relationships with landowners and others.

2. Rights of way often cross fields which may be supporting crops. Every effort should be made to walk in single file in such a way as to minimize crop damage.

3. There are instances of farmers erecting fences, occasionally electrified (low voltage) or barbed, across the right of way to contain the movement of livestock. While in my experience such activities are encountered only occasionally care should be taken in negotiating such obstacles and it is suggested that such instances should be reported back to the Rights of Way Department at Lancashire County Council.

4. Especially in winter, fields can be difficult to negotiate, particularly near gates where livestock congregate. Conditions can be very muddy indeed and Wellington boots are often an essential alternative to walking boots. For each walk guidance is given on suitable footwear.

5. In summer, some stiles and other access points into and out of fields can become hazardous due to the growth of nettles, brambles and hawthorn hedges. It is useful to carry in the backpack a pair of gardening gloves to handle such vegetation safely. It is also advisable, if wearing shorts, to carry a stick to beat down nettles in particular.

6. For those of you who are wary of farm animals just bear in mind that cows and sheep may follow you occasionally but only because they think you may have some food. If you turn and walk towards them they will stop and back away. Even when a herd of cattle are gathered at a gate required for access they will disperse on approaching them. Dogs can sometimes sound intimidating but usually they will keep their distance. Larger dogs are nearly always chained; after all, the last thing farmers will want is to risk a claim from someone bitten by their dog. Usually, the most aggressive animals encountered are geese although, in my experience, rarely.

7. It is preferable to open and close a gate in the proper manner but, if that is not possible, then it may be necessary to climb over. There is little alternative. Under no circumstances should gates be left open where there is livestock in a field.

8. If bringing a dog then they should be kept on a lead at all times. To disregard this will incur the displeasure of farmers and road users alike.

9. It is advisable to carry a map, preferably a 1:25000 Pathfinder (numbers 658, 668, 678 and 679 cover nearly all the walks) or, failing that, a 1:50000 Landranger (map 102 covers the whole area) although these are not so accurate for checking the rights of way. A compass is useful for all but the shortest walks and, likewise, it is recommended to bring waterproofs, warm clothing and some food and drink to cover all eventualities.

10. Please exercise great care when walking close to barbed wire or other sharp edges, especially where the ground is sloping and/or muddy thereby increasing the risk of slipping or stumbling. Extra care is required with children who may be oblivious to the dangers.

Introduction

11. Common sense should be exercised when in the countryside. Therefore, guard against fire risks, fasten gates, take home all litter and protect wildlife, plants and trees. If you find yourself lost in a farmyard just ask for assistance. This is preferable to wandering around a farm and you will generally find that farmers are helpful.

12. The availability of buses and trams is referred to in the most general of terms. Because the information is liable to change it is essential to contact the relevant operating authority for the latest information. Tourist Information offices usually stock timetables.

13. All the walks have been checked for accuracy with the Rights of Way department at Lancashire County Council in 2003 but I have had to make a number of amendments to account for changes since they were previously checked two years ago. Please be aware that the countryside is constantly changing so beware of hedges that may have been moved, fences that may have been erected and new housing development. It is at times like these when a map can provide invaluable assistance and, if necessary, help to work out an alternative route.

14. There are instances where signs have been erected to guide walkers along a certain route but it should be noted that, while such directions may appear logical, they may not represent the legal right of way as used in this book.

15. For those of you who are easily put off by the hazards of walking then can I suggest that you contain your walking to late spring and summer when ground conditions are likely to be more favourable. Also avoid walking after periods of heavy or persistent rain and when it is windy otherwise it will only serve to confirm the convictions you already hold! For inexperienced walkers it is suggested that some of the smaller walks be tackled first and in the information panels I try to give an indication of what to expect on each walk.

The Farming Year

Most of the walks within this book pass through farms and fields and it is easy to be lulled into thinking that they are there for the benefit of walkers while, at the same time, harbouring the secret wish that they didn't smell quite so much! The farmer, who has to make a living while producing our food, will no doubt have his or her own wish list including more respectful house-keeping on the part of walkers: closing gates, keeping dogs under close control, and keeping to the right of way. In the introduction I have attempted to give guidance on matters that would help the relationship between farmer and walker but I thought it might be useful to give a brief summary of farming activities during the year to help engender a better understanding of life on the farm.

Spring: A particularly sensitive time of the year as the sowing and planting of early potatoes, cereals, sugar beet and main-crop potatoes takes place during late February to April. The last harvests of winter vegetables such as swedes and broccolis is completed by March. This is also the time for lambing and calving. Early lambing begins in January and continues at least into May while calving is mainly confined to March and April. Cattle are brought out to graze from March, when the grass begins to grow, until October. The first silage is cut during the spring.

Summer: The harvest season begins with new potatoes, fruit, oilseed rape, peas, winter wheat, spring barley and sweet corn all being gathered in. The second silage cut will also have taken place, weather permitting.

Autumn: Ploughing and cultivating becomes an important task from late August to the end of November while the sowing and planting of crops such as oilseed rape, winter barley and winter wheat resumes during, roughly, the same period. A third silage cut may be taken while harvesting continues with field beans, fruit, main-crop potatoes, carrots, sugar beet and cauliflowers throughout the season. By the end of November cattle are housed for the winter.

Winter: The time of the year when sprouts and cabbage are harvested and when basic maintenance to buildings, machinery, hedges, fences and ditches is undertaken in readiness for another year. Fertilisers and pesticides are generally applied to crops when necessary, during the year, according to the stage of growth.

WALK 1

Fleetwood

Get to know one of the most interesting towns in Lancashire

Distance:	2¾ or 5½ miles
Start:	From the North Euston Hotel, between the lighthouses, at the north end of the town. Grid reference: 338485
Map:	OS Pathfinder 658; OS Landranger 102
Time allowed:	1¼ hours, 2½ hours
Conditions and difficulties:	Normal footwear should be quite sufficient for this town walk
Facilities:	There are all the normal range of facilities associated with a town including public toilets opposite the entrance to the North Euston Hotel
Public transport:	There is a regular tram service from Blackpool to the terminus, opposite the North Euston Hotel, and a regular bus service from Preston and Lancaster

1 Fleetwood is one of the earliest examples of a planned town and it came about through the vision of Sir Peter Hesketh-Fleetwood of Rossall Hall and the designs of his architect, Decimus Burton. The North Euston Hotel, with its fine portico of fluted Doric columns, was a reminder of the connection with London's old Euston station. Opened in 1841 its first manager, Xenon Vantini, had been a courier for Napoleon Bonaparte. From here walk across the road to the promenade and turn left towards the pier. Note the old naval mine once used as an offensive weapon in the Second World War and now serving an alternative use as a collection box. Beyond the pier follow the path round to the right towards the beach. As we do so we pass the first of many small beach bungalows that can be hired at a very reasonable price, making the prospect of a day at the seaside all the more pleasurable. Looking out to sea at this point the structure that can be seen about two miles from the shore is the Wyre Light, guarding the entrance to the tortuous channel. It is no longer used. Now we pass behind the rear of the swimming pool and the Marine Hall, with its bowling greens and gardens, until, just beyond another group of beach bungalows, turn left if following the shorter walk, away from the sea, along a short road that leads up to the Esplanade. If you wish to continue by the sea follow the instructions under 6 below.

Cross over the Esplanade and enter the gardens at the base of the Mount. Take the path up to this highest land-based point in the area from where there are good views out to sea. Looking inland one can see the pattern of roads radiating from here in accordance with the original design for the town. Before reaching the mast, beyond the craft centre, turn right along a path descending through the park towards the entrance gate, a building of sandstone blocks with a tunnel through the middle leading us out on to Mount Road. Our way forward from here is straight ahead along the broad, tree-lined, London Street that leads us directly to the main shopping thoroughfare, Lord Street, recognizable by the tram

Fylde Coast and Country Walks

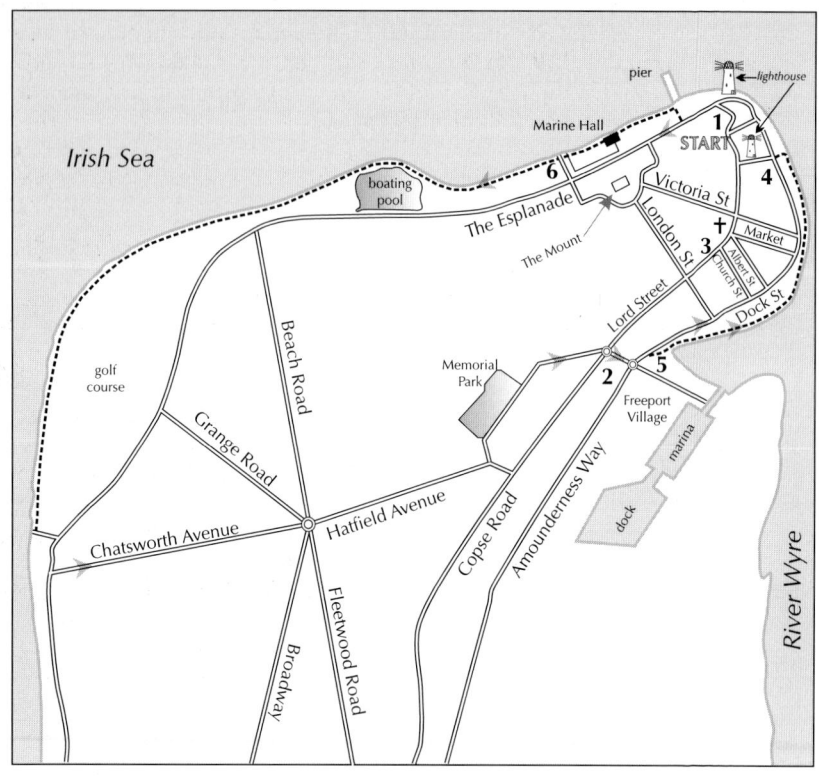

lines. Here is the oldest tramway in Britain still in use and the only one of any size that still operates the old type of tram that was once a feature of the larger cities. Turn right here and continue to the roundabout at Fisherman's Walk. Note the Lofthouse Clock on the right, erected in memory to a member of the Lofthouse family, owners of one of Fleetwood's best-known companies, Fisherman's Friend. From Lord Street turn left at the roundabout into Station Road.

2 The name of this road is a reminder that, at the far end of the road, once stood Wyre Dock station. Occupying the former station site is another roundabout. We shall turn left here but, before doing so, go straight across to Anchorage Road with Mariner's Quay, a housing development, on the left and the Freeport retail and leisure complex over to the right. Continue for a short distance until the road ends at gates. Just beyond are the lock gates at the entrance to Fleetwood docks on the right, part of which is now a marina for pleasure craft. It is worth considering just how busy this point must have been at the height of the fishing industry, now a shadow of its former self. Return now to the roundabout and turn right into Dock Street where several of the oldest buildings are sited. As an alternative there is a public right of way beside the harbour and, should you prefer this route, follow the instructions in 5 below.

Walk 1: Fleetwood

On reaching the far corner of the junction with Mount Street, by the Fleetwood Arms, note the small cottage-type terraced houses built to accommodate those employed at the docks and on the boats. Then, at the junction with London Street, look to the far end for a view of the Mount. Further along on the same side, opposite the entrance to the ferry terminal, is one of the town's original stone block buildings, at the far corner of Kemp Street. This is just one of several buildings of similar vintage that we now encounter including, at Warren Street, Pennine View, formerly the Crown Hotel that opened in 1841. It was the fifth hotel to be built in Fleetwood during a time of optimism. Across to the right is the site of the original terminus for the Preston and Wyre Railway, opened on 15 July 1840. A little further is Church Street, once an important shopping street that led to the station. Here we turn left to return to Lord Street and the parish church of St Peter's, erected in 1841.

3 Turn right into Lord Street to arrive at the modest Albert Square and the Rowntree Clock Tower, erected in memory of the town's first female mayor. It stands on the site of the former parish pump that provided water for the local residents. Two roads diverge to the right from Albert Square and we take the second of these, Adelaide Street, that leads us back to Dock Street. It is well worth calling in at Fleetwood Market, however, which can be seen on the left. Originally opened in 1840, it gained its covered hall in 1890. At the far end of Adelaide Street turn left into Queen's Terrace. Further views of the Mount can be seen along Victoria Street, the next road on the left, before we encounter the Fleetwood Museum housed in the old Custom House, immediately recognizable by its prominent portico. On the right is the site of the later railway terminus, re-sited to reduce the distance between train and ship, while on the left is the imposing Queen's Terrace, with its central pediment and cast iron balconies, designed by Decimus Burton. Now turn left into Pharos Street.

4 Immediately in front of us stands the Pharos Lighthouse, a tall, impressive circular stone tower with a gallery at the top. Turn right into Upper Lune Street and then, looking ahead, another lighthouse known as Lower Lighthouse will be seen. Both lighthouses were built in 1840 and designed by Decimus Burton. It is now out of use but the significance of these structures was their juxtaposition. They were, in fact, an aid to navigation for shipping approaching the town because, by aligning the two towers one in front of the other, a straight course could be navigated towards the port. Proceed towards the lighthouse on the seafront to reach the starting point once again, outside the North Euston Hotel. It is worth a look around the small park opposite as it contains some relics of the past including a cannon that was once displayed on the seafront and fired as a salute during Queen Victoria's visit here. It is also worth crossing to the promenade to look at the touching sculpture entitled 'Welcome Home', created by Anita Lafford and dedicated to the lives of local fishermen and their families.

5 Having turned into Dock Street take the first right turn again towards the quayside and follow the made-up road alongside the Wyre. At the end of this road take a path to the left of railings and continue between the river and the huge vehicle park on the left. Look out for the large sandstone blocks in the quayside wall.

Fylde Coast and Country Walks

'Welcome Home' by Anita Lafford

Walk 1: Fleetwood

This building material was used in much of Fleetwood's early public buildings. As we round the bend look out for Knott End across the mouth of the estuary. Some of its features are seen at close hand on the walks from that town. Before crossing the bridge (which spans the access road to the ferries) it should be noted that the path ahead cannot be used when boats are arriving or departing. Once over the other side, continue alongside the ferry berth. At the end of the perimeter fence on the left note the impressive classical Queen's Terrace across the road but continue, close to the river, until level with the far edge of the building. Now turn left to cross the road and head for the lighthouse as directed under 4 above.

6 Continue along the outer promenade past the miniature golf course and boating pool. At low tide groups of people can often be seen looking intently at the sands. It is likely that they will be looking for lugworms, used by fishermen. For those who are interested in learning about coastal plants there is an abundance of vegetation to see during the growing season from this path. Indeed, one of the pleasures of walking along this section is being at close quarters to the beach, unlike much of the Fylde coast which is protected by the huge concrete sea-defence walls. It appears that there is little defence against wind-blown sand, however, which has formed substantial banks on our left all but obliterating the original fence-line, parts of which can still be seen. The promenade eventually bends round slightly to the left and, a little further, we pass the Coastguard Station in the vicinity of Rossall Point. For birdwatchers this is an area where some of the rarer seabirds can be seen occasionally, blown off course, and where shore birds often congregate. By now the grassy bank on the left has given way to a concrete wall, marking the boundary of Fleetwood Golf Course. As the path curves round to the south it should be possible to see Blackpool Tower and the North Pier in the distance. Approaching the end of the golf links look out for a broad, made-up path and turn left to the road. Then turn right and, at the first junction, turn left into Chatsworth Avenue.

We now start the return journey to the town centre but note the grassy mound on the left, a remnant of the old coastal defence that could also be seen at the southern end of the golf course. The first house on the left is styled Ye Old Pump House and is the only house along this straight road that can be regarded as of pre-war vintage. Press ahead to eventually reach a busy roundabout. Go directly across at this point onto Hatfield Avenue which continues in the same direction until reaching a right-hand bend. Here turn left into Nelson Road to pass the side of the Memorial Park, dedicated to those who died in the two great wars. At the far end of the park turn right into Warrenhurst Road opposite the imposing gates to the park. The road leads us to the Lofthouse Memorial Clock (see under 1) from where we cross over the tram tracks and the roundabout into Station Road and follow the instructions under 2 above.

WALK 2

Thornton

A range of options is available from the Wyre Estuary Country Park alongside the river and returning either via Marsh Mill or rural by-ways

Distance:	From 2 to 6 miles
Start:	From the Wyre Estuary Country Park, east of Thornton village. Grid reference: 355432
Map:	OS Pathfinder 658; OS Landranger 102
Time allowed:	Between 1 and 3 hours
Conditions and difficulties:	Walking boots are recommended
Facilities:	Refreshments and toilet facilities at the Wyre Ecology Centre together with plentiful car parking spaces and picnic tables. If walking to Marsh Mill, there is a variety of public houses and shops en route, especially in the vicinity of Station Road and the windmill
Public transport:	There are regular bus services from Cleveleys

1 From the car park proceed towards the estuary, following the spine road round to the right and take the signposted path (Riverside Path) along the estuary towards the pylon. Behind us is the former ICI complex at Hillhouse; it was ICI who funded the conversion of this former tipping site into the attractive country park we see today. Briefly we pass a reedy section on our left and then, further on, the path bends round and under power cables, beyond which it meets another path from a higher level on the right. The different levels are a reminder that the gently rolling hummocks on both sides of the Wyre are moraine, or debris, deposited by huge glaciers as they retreated northwards at the end of the Ice Age (five thousand years ago). The geological term for these low-lying hills is drumlins.

A little further on, a signposted path sets off at right-angles to Underbank Road at a small picnic site. There was once a small cottage on the site known as Cockle Hall. Nearby was a jetty from where a ferry service operated until the 1930s to Wardley Pool, across the river, close to where Wardley Hotel is situated. Both Wardleys and Skippool (encountered later on) pre-date Fleetwood as ports for this area and, from the early eighteenth century, they both experienced an upsurge in activity, justifying the building of warehouses and quays. Goods landed at Wardleys were shipped across to Skippool for onward transportation by cart to destinations such as Poulton and Kirkham. There was even shipbuilding at both ports, though mainly at Wardleys where the largest ship to be completed was the *Hope* at 415 tons in the 1830s. As we round the next bend, the Blackpool and Fleetwood Yacht Club can be seen by the shore, lined with boats. The path continues to bend round westwards and then almost to the north west until, arriving at a creek, a junction is reached where a path branches off to the right. If following this shorter route (2 miles round trip – allow about an hour), take

Walk 2: Thornton

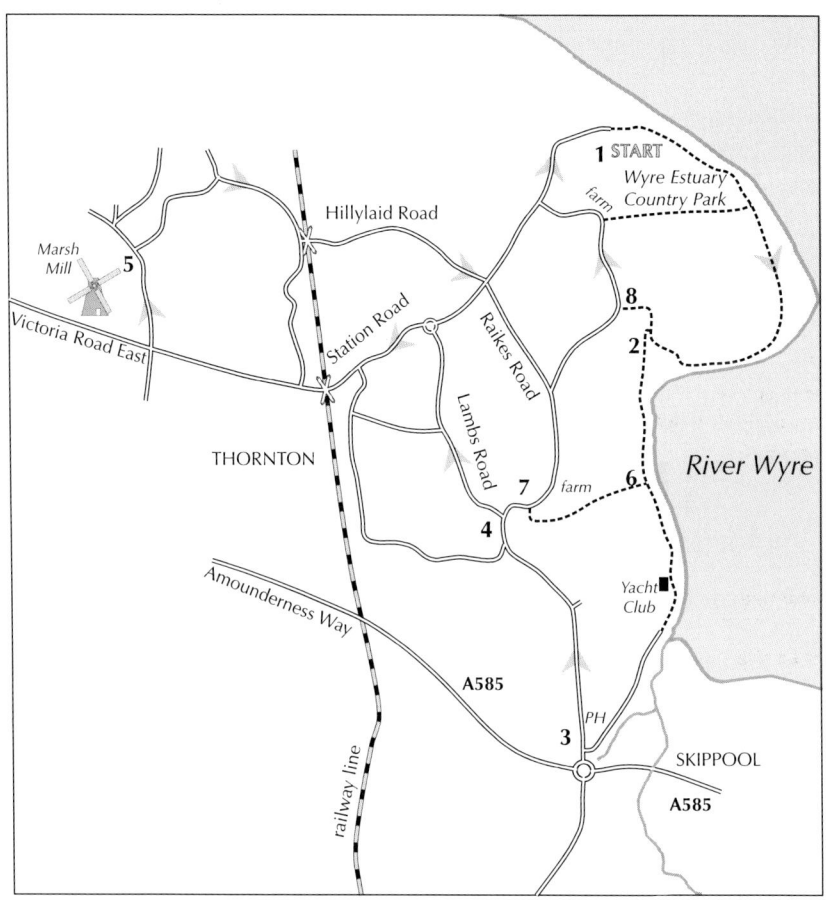

the path through the gate, to the left of the vehicular access, and proceed along the track, bounded by hedgerows. Continue round a sharp left-hand bend and follow the track to the T-junction on a bend. Turn right into the lane and return as directed in section 8.

2 If continuing along the estuary, cross over the creek and follow the path to reach the first of more than one hundred wooden jetties allowing private access to boats either undergoing restoration or repair, or simply moored at the riverbank. They vary from dinghies and yachts to small trawlers and, like the jetties themselves, vary in condition. Remember, though, that they are not for public access and may be dangerous. While the boats at the end of the jetties naturally attract interest, keep a lookout for a public footpath sign pointing towards Little Thornton. If returning, via the stile and steps on the right, please follow the directions from 6 below.

Continue past the seemingly endless rows of jetties until reaching the club house of the Blackpool and Fleetwood Yacht Club, established in 1906. The

Fylde Coast and Country Walks

slipways lie to our left as we continue ahead to join a made-up road. Passing River House on our right we soon reach Skippool Creek where there is a picnic site on the right. In this vicinity was the Fylde's busiest port, particularly busy during the seventeenth and eighteenth centuries but declining quickly with the completion of the port of Fleetwood. This may be a suitable spot for a break but, otherwise, continue to follow the road round to the right until the last of the jetties is passed with the main Fleetwood road, the A585, visible beyond. It is now a short distance along Wyre Road to the junction with Skippool Road.

3 Turn right here and, ideally, cross over to the other side where the pavement is broader. Sheep can be seen grazing in the fields but one wonders for how long these green pastures can withstand the pressures for housing development. A little further, on the right, look out for two substantial gateposts, one of which bears the name Illawalla. Here was the entrance to a house that yielded to the developers, as the small housing estate bears witness, but the original house was of interest in that it was the home of a famous music hall star, Vesta Tilley, a male impersonator. Towards the end of its life the house was also used as a film set for Ken Russell's film *Valentino*, starring Rudolph Nureyev.

The road now bends to the left, skirting the boundary wall of Ashley House. Shortly after the next right-hand bend look out for Raikes Road on the right. This is the last chance for an early return to our starting point as we shall now be moving inland towards Marsh Mill. So, if you choose to take Raikes Road, it is just a short distance, past one or two pretty cottages and a public footpath sign on the right, from where you should continue and follow the directions under 7 below.

4 Passing Raikes Road continue, along what has now become Lambs Road, round to the left. It begins to rise towards Stanah Primary School, ahead on the right, before making a loop around to the left along Station Road towards Thornton village. Eventually a level crossing is reached, by the remains of what was Thornton station (the platforms are still in situ). Passenger trains ceased to run a long time ago but the very occasional freight train still ventures up the line. Beyond the crossing continue past the centre of the village, along Victoria Road East as far as the traffic lights, adjacent to the War Memorial. Turn right and soon the 70 foot high Marsh Mill comes into view. It is little more than 400 yards to the mill complex on the left, dominated by the only working example of a windmill on the Fylde. It stands at the front of a pleasant shopping complex of colonnades, arches, cobbles and courtyards.

5 On leaving Marsh Mill turn left along the main road but then, almost immediately, cross over to turn right into Woodlands Avenue. The road curves round to the left and right before reaching a junction at the far end. Note Trunnah Farm, now the last house on the right but, at one time, surrounded by fields. Turn right at the junction and pass the shops. After about 400 yards look out for a level crossing over Hillylaid Road that forks away to the left. Follow this road, over the former Fleetwood branch line, to pass a substantial development of modern housing. Eventually, on reaching crossroads, turn left into

Walk 2: Thornton

Marsh Mill. The only working mill on the Fylde

Stanah Road. Continue all the way to our starting point at the car park, turning sharp right beforehand at Kneps Farm, now a caravan site.

6 Having left the Wyre and the jetties via a stile and a flight of steps, we reach a field above the trees. Keep along the left-hand edge of the field until it reaches a brow. This is a good point to stop and look back to take in extensive views of this section of the meandering river. Shard Bridge can be seen clearly to the right while the Lancashire fells are visible in the distance. Keep on along the field edge to reach a track leading to a farm. It passes by the side of the farmyard leading us, straight on, to Woodhouse Road. Proceed past Ilex House on the right and, just beyond a right-hand bend, look out for steps on either side of the road leading up to stiles. Take the stile on the right, at the top of the steps, and walk along the left-hand edge of the field. It is just a short distance to a stile in the far left-hand corner which gives us access to Raikes Road at the point where we join those walking via Skippool Creek. Turn right here.

7 At the first left-hand bend we pass the entrance to Thornton Hall Farm on the right and then I commend you to soak up the very pleasant rural tranquillity of this corner of the Fylde. Yes, there is the sound of traffic over to the left but the feeling of being away from it all is, nevertheless, quite compelling. It is to be hoped that the local planning authority resists all attempts to develop one of the few remaining rural backwaters in this part of the Fylde.

In time we are joined by a ditch on our right as a junction is approached, with a house in the middle of the fork. At the junction take the right fork where there is a bench on the right that may be a suitable stop for a refreshment break. Further on, as the lane begins to lose height and the banks on both sides become deeper, the name of Underbank Road becomes understandable. Now we could be miles from civilisation as we are surrounded by trees, hedges and fields. At a left-hand bend the ditch on the right veers away and we pass a farm track leading directly to the river. This is the track that, earlier, provided the quickest return to the car park.

8 Continue past the former farm cottages on the right and rise to a brow before passing under power cables. At a left-hand corner stands Stanah Farm and, along the next stretch, we pass Stanah Hill Farm cottages. On the right can be seen remnants of a cobbled wall, adding to the air of rural rusticity, and once again I feel the need to reiterate the hope that this small portion of genuine rural charm in this part of the Fylde is retained for the benefit of the local population.

All too soon we reach a T-junction with Stanah Road and turn right along River Road towards Knep Farm Holiday Home and Touring Park, and then right again, passing the flood control station before entering the Country Park.

WALK 3

Cleveleys and Thornton

A walk of contrasts; of coast and estuary, of the seaside resort of Cleveleys, dating largely from the nineteenth century, and the village of Thornton, recorded in the Domesday Book

Distance:	2½ or 8½ miles
Start:	From the junction of the north and south promenades where they meet Victoria Road West at the roundabout. Grid reference: 313429
Map:	OS Pathfinder 658; OS Landranger 102
Time allowed:	1¼ or 4 hours
Conditions and difficulties:	Walking boots should prove quite sufficient for the longer walk and normal shoes for the shorter stroll
Facilities:	Shops and eating places in abundance in Cleveleys plus the facilities at Wyre Estuary Country Park (about half-way round on the longer walk) including toilets
Public transport:	There are regular tram and bus services from Blackpool and Fleetwood and buses from Thornton and Poulton

1 Park along either Promenade North or South (there will be naturally more space available outside the peak summer months) and walk to the clock tower on the roundabout, close to the promenade at the end of the main shopping street, Victoria Road West. In fact, it is along this shopping street that we must begin our walk, making our way inland from the sea to the main traffic lights. Turn left here and follow the tram route north as far as the parish church of St Andrew's. On reaching the church cross the road, over the tram lines, and continue in the same direction turning right into Stockdove Way (note Cleveleys Library on the other side of the road just before reaching our turn), the next turn after West Drive. Some houses along this road featured in a cottage exhibition of 1906, noteworthy because of the involvement of a young Edward Lutyens in the design. Continue along this tree-lined road, over the crossroads, and follow the road round the bend to the right to join West Drive.

Turn left and soon cross over North Drive to continue through an attractive residential area along West Drive. Just beyond the junction the road bends a little to the left. Note the circular stone posts marking the entrance to Holmefield Avenue and, further on, after the road bends again to the left, look out for Wardle Drive, between two tall circular stone posts and leading directly into a wood. This is an unexpected and very pleasant surprise, especially as it is in the middle of a suburb. As we approach a kissing gate, leading into the wood, it is like discovering an oasis in the middle of a desert. What is so delightful is that it looks as if this small natural woodland has been here for a long time and still remains unspoilt. A pond is passed on the left and then the path takes a sharp right-hand turn to arrive at a junction of paths. Turn left here to pass another

Fylde Coast and Country Walks

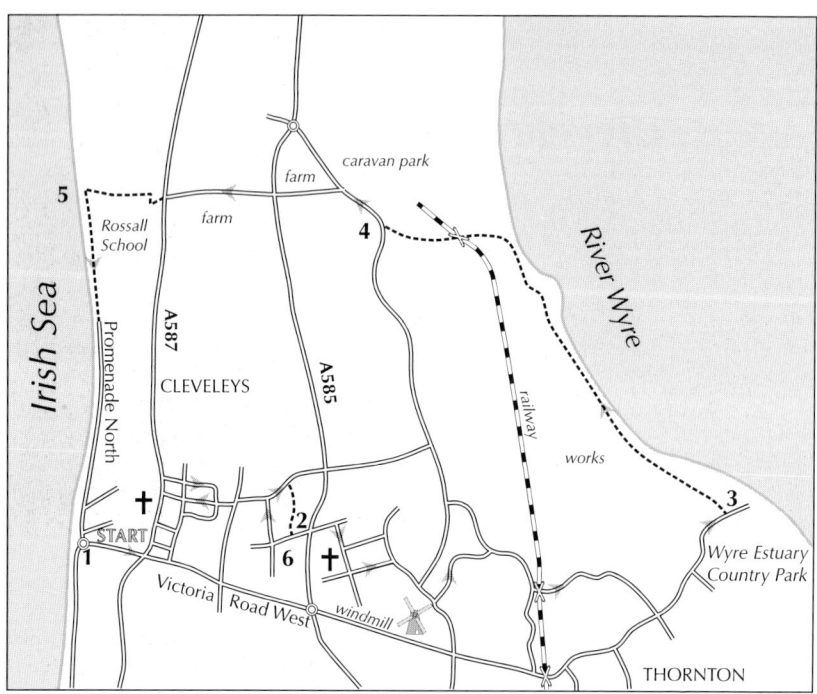

pool on the left. Soon another kissing gate, between two more circular stone posts, is reached. If wishing to follow the short route back to Cleveleys turn right and follow the directions under 6 below. Otherwise, turn left here and continue ahead, ignoring Seniors Drive on the left to reach the main road to Fleetwood.

2 In a very short space of time we have moved from a quiet pastoral oasis in a residential area of Cleveleys to the busy main road that effectively separates Thornton from Cleveleys. Cross over the road at a pedestrian crossing and onwards in the same direction, passing a small field on the left, and continue along Linden Avenue, a short distance before turning first right into Meadows Avenue. As we pass a cemetery with its open graveyard (no walls) look out for a curious conifer whose trunk is almost in the shape of a question mark. Thornton Parish Church (Christ Church) stands on the right with its free-standing campanile. Turn left beyond the church into Church Road and continue past a modern housing development. Keep going until Church Road bends to the right at which point the windmill in Thornton should become visible. At the junction with the main road turn right towards the windmill. It is worth calling at the Marsh Mill Village development of cobbled walkways, squares and arcades, not least because the windmill is the only working example in the North. Built in 1794 by Ralph Slater it continued in operation until 1922. After this time it was used as a cafe and furniture store until its restoration. In case you are wondering why it is called Marsh Mill it is simply because the surrounding land was subjected to regular flooding at one time.

Walk 3: Cleveleys and Thornton

A woodland refuge in a residential area of Cleveleys

Having visited the mill turn left onto the main road and cross over to find Woodland Avenue. Proceeding along this road note the brook on the left that is culverted under the main road. This is a pleasant meandering road with the brook visible further on. There is a pavement on one side only for the majority of its length. At the far end note Trunnah Farm on the right with its cobbled boundary wall. Its fields will, no doubt, have provided the land on which the surrounding residential area was built. At the end of the road turn right, across Rossendale Road, and then past the shops. Keep going but as we cross Bancroft Avenue on the right look ahead to a junction where we need to turn left to cross the old Fleetwood railway line at a level crossing.

We are now on Hillylaid Road where modern housing development predominates. Eventually we cross a brook and, just beyond, is Brook Farm (the name is set in stone, high up in the brickwork, bearing a date of 1892). It is one of the few buildings of any age along this road and gives a clue as to the previous land use not that long ago. On finally reaching a substantial crossroads, with a modern church across the road on the left-hand side, turn left into Stanah Road. Shortly, it appears as if we are to enter open countryside with the appearance of a large sloping field on the right but, just as we round the bend, another modern housing development appears on the left. Further on, Stanah Road turns off to the right into unspoilt countryside but we must continue straight ahead into what becomes River Road which eventually bends round to the right at Kneps Farm, now a caravan park. On passing a water control station we enter the Wyre Estuary Country Park. There is an information centre and toilets on the right and food and drink are available.

From the information centre return down the short flight of steps and turn right onto the access road into the park but immediately look out for a footpath sign

- 17 -

on the left in the trees at the nearside corner of the car park on the left. This enclosed path, signposted Fleetwood Road, soon passes by creeks alongside the banks of the Wyre. The path then passes above a caravan site along the top of a flood control embankment for the Wyre. Soon we draw level with the first buildings of the former ICI complex. Across the Wyre, at this point, is the hamlet of Staynall surrounded by farmland and with farms sited on the low-lying drumlins that provide such good views on a clear day. Eventually the track crosses pipelines which, very accommodatingly, dip underground to facilitate this move. As we approach the tall factory chimney, which has been a landmark for many years, note the river Wyre which is almost at its broadest. Fleetwood and Knott End at either side of the mouth of the river can be seen ahead. When almost level with the chimney note the steps leading down to a jetty, a small pipeline emerging from the mud and the remnants of a huge pipeline a few yards further on. The track here follows the course of the former works railway by the site of the old Ammonia Soda Works. Soon our right of way veers to the left and right to maintain its previous course but a little inland to accommodate a large creek where the remaining stumps of old jetties, supported on wooden piers, can be seen. The truncated remains of a huge pipe, that was once connected to the reservoir inside the perimeter fence, emerge from the banking. The path curves round at the far end of the reservoir to approach gates. Just when it appears that we may have reached a dead end a footpath sign points left along a path between paling fences. Immediately to the north of here the Burn Naze Salt Works was established by the Fleetwood Salt Company, with a pipeline across the Wyre to the saltfields of Preesall. This is where the salt and brine industry on the Fylde began and which developed into the ICI complex.

Now turn left along the Wyre Way. Over to our right ran the original course of the railway to Fleetwood until it was re-routed inland because of continuing instability caused by the marshlands. Eventually the path meets the former Fleetwood line near its present most northerly extent. Cross the line to a stile on the far side. Then climb a small flight of steps to join a pleasant narrow enclosed path on a bank. On a hot summer's day the shade will, no doubt, be very welcome. The path continues, enclosed for some way, passing industrial land on the left before eventually reaching the boundary of a large caravan site on the right. At a stile it eventually emerges onto a track and, from here, continues the short distance to a main road. Note the outline of Rossall School in the distance ahead.

4 Turn right now and soon we pass the entrance to Cala Gran caravan park. As we walk alongside the caravan park look out for a road on the left, signposted to Farmer Parr's Animal World. The entrance to the farm is immediately on our right as we enter the road and, further on to the right, is the farmyard. There is a country feel to this road with fields on either side but it is too flat and there are not enough trees to give the feeling that we are genuinely away from it all. In any event, the traffic on the road ahead of us is a reminder that this is, now, an urban environment. A variety of animals may be seen in the fields here and, further to the right, it is possible to pick out the Statue of Eros, erected on a roundabout in 1999 and funded by the Lofthouse Foundation. Continue now to Amounderness Way, which can be very busy, and cross over to Rossall Lane.

Initially there are fields on either side and the Nautical College further to the

Walk 3: Cleveleys and Thornton

Industry on the Wyre

right. We pass Fleetwood Farm on the left and encounter a housing estate on the right. At the tramlines by Rossall Lane Halt on the right continue a little further to the main road and cross straight over and continue for a further 50 yards until reaching a broad track on the right leading to a recreation area and tennis courts. Keep going until reaching a car park area but, without entering the parking area, swing to the left with the track to reach a kissing gate. Now resume in a straight line with open fields on the right, sometimes with cattle grazing, and Rossall School on the left. Head straight for an embankment. We pass a cobbled wall on the left and then farm buildings which appear to be part of the school complex. Maybe the cobbled wall was part of the original hall. A gate at the far end leads up to the coastal embankment. Before moving on, however, it is worth bearing in mind that there are interesting historic connections at Rossall.

The school was adapted from the home of the Allen family, one of whom, William Allen, was appointed Canon of York by Mary Tudor. As a devout Catholic he was later forced into exile where he founded an English college at Douai. There young priests were trained for missionary work in England but he achieved notoriety when he became linked with plots to remove protestant Queen Elizabeth. As a result he was forced to spend the rest of his life in exile making the occasional secret visit to Rossall where he entertained, amongst others, the prominent Jesuit leader, Edmund Campion. Allen achieved the status of Cardinal before he died in 1594 but, by then, Rossall had become home to the Fleetwood family and later to the Heskeths. It was Peter Hesketh who invested his money in the development of Fleetwood with the help of architect, Decimus Burton. He adopted the name of the town and became Hesketh-Fleetwood but the costs involved in building a new town and port became such a burden that he was forced to sell the house and Rossall School was founded in 1844. Little of the original home now survives.

5 Turn left, on reaching the embankment, to return to Cleveleys. Note the chapel at the far end of the school on our left and, if looking over from the promenade,

Fylde Coast and Country Walks

Designed by Lutyens, Cleveleys

one can see the former raised, protective grassy embankment around the playing fields that once acted as the sea defences. Continue along Rossall promenade all the way to Cleveleys between houses on the left and the Irish Sea on the right. Note the Jubilee Gardens on the left, marked by pillars on the road at both ends of the park. It was opened by Lord Stanley in 1937. Beyond Jubilee Gardens look out for the car park off North Promenade where there are toilet facilities and beach huts. Soon we reach the centre once again with the clock tower and its shelter on the roundabout at the entrance to the main shopping street, our starting point.

6 Having turned right into Linden Close, consisting of large houses set in substantial grounds, continue to where it meets Holmefield Avenue and turn right. Another entrance to the wood is past on the right as we continue to the circular pillars seen earlier on either side of the road. Turn left now along West Drive and cross over North Drive. Soon we shall see Stockdove Way again on the right but, this time, continue straight down West Drive where more of the houses that featured in the Cottage Exhibition will be seen. Indeed, the date of the exhibition, 1906, is inscribed on at least two of the houses on the left. Soon we arrive at the tramlines and the main Rossall Road. Cross the road and turn left and continue, beyond the mini roundabout, to the traffic lights in the town centre. Turn right into Victoria Road West, past the main shops, to the far end where the roundabout will be seen with the clock tower and shelter.

WALK 4

North of Blackpool

A linear walk, using the tram in one direction. It is walking in particular that reveals just how high the land can reach above sea level. Choose a clear and calm day for best results.

Distance:	2¾/4 miles
Start:	From Norbreck Road at its junction with Queen's Promenade, next to the Norbreck Castle Hotel. Grid reference: 310406
Map:	OS Pathfinder 658/678; OS Landranger 102
Time allowed:	1½ hours or 2 hours (excluding the tram ride)
Conditions and difficulties:	Unless you have chosen a wild and windy day at high tide normal shoes should be sufficient. Do take binoculars if you have them
Facilities:	All the usual facilities associated with Blackpool and its suburbs
Public transport:	There is a regular tram service from Blackpool and Fleetwood and also bus services

1 From the suggested starting point walk to the nearest tram stop opposite the Norbreck Castle Hotel. Walk to the North Pier by all means but I have suggested the tram because a ride on one is an experience in itself. The Blackpool tramway system is the only original one in the country and, consequently, offers the only insight into a way of travelling that, apart from at Blackpool, disappeared in 1960. Take the tram as far as the North Pier and, assuming that you have not succumbed to the temptations of the shops and leisure activities, start walking back towards Cleveleys. At this point Blackpool Tower is immediately behind us, a structure unique in Britain and impressive, however many times you see it.

2 The stark white monument ahead of us is also impressive. Unveiled on 11 November 1923 it is a lasting memorial to those who died in both World Wars and subsequent conflicts. There is a choice of two routes now but from the higher promenade, just below the hotel ahead, there is more to see and the views to the west extend to a further horizon. As we pass the Metropole, the only hotel on the seaward side of the coast road, note the impressive balustrade in front of the hotel that offers shelter at the lower level. It bears the date 1912 when Princess Louise visited Blackpool to open this section of the sea front known, appropriately, as Princess Parade and where the first illuminated display was sited. As the promenade bends to the right look ahead along the coastline, surprisingly high above the sea in parts. The tram tracks close in on us and, for the time being, our way is beside the tracks. Hotels line one side of this part of the route, all the way to Gynn Square. There are attractive semi-circular embellishments to the promenade along this section opposite the tram stops. They are supported by pillars that form colonnades at the lower promenade, offering shelter at that level at the same time. At the Warley Road tram stop look right, up Warley Road, to

Fylde Coast and Country Walks

Cliff top and cabin lift, Blackpool

appreciate just how hilly this part of the town really is. Soon the promenade curves to the right towards Gynn Square, now marked by a roundabout!

You will notice that we have been walking gradually downhill to Gynn Square and that is because, before this part of Blackpool was developed, the cliffs were breached by a stream at this point. Now the stream is culverted but there is an outlet to the sea here. The modern Gynn Inn is situated at the far side of the roundabout from the sea whereas the original eighteenth-century inn stood closer to the modern brick shelter in front of us where the original Blackpool and Fleetwood Tramway terminated. It was only after its purchase in 1919 by Blackpool Corporation that the tramway was connected to the section running along the Golden Mile. To the left of the shelter steps provide access to the lower promenade and from the lower level one can appreciate the semi-circular shelters supported on sets of double pillars with balustrades above.

3 Return to the upper promenade and proceed to the gardens that separate us from the tram tracks. At the entrance to this garden there is a large stone pillar (there is another across the road) with a plaque, donated by entertainers and people of the Fylde, honouring three police officers who died during a sea rescue attempt on 5 January 1983. There is now a steady climb passing more hotels including the appropriately named Cliff Hotel. Near the summit of the promenade there are cliff walks and a small promontory near the top of the cliffs. Across the road is Uncle Tom's Cabin, a reminder that the original once stood on the cliffs here. It was Blackpool's first place of amusement but was demolished when the cliffs on which it stood began to crumble. Looking down the next road on the right one can see the water tower at Warbreck Reservoir, a landmark for miles around. A little further is the cabin lift, in modern brick with attractive classical ornamentation. The rocky cliffs give way now to grassy slopes as we dip slightly before rising to another crest which, like the summit at the cabin lift, is about

– 22 –

Walk 4: North of Blackpool

the highest point on the Fylde coast. From this section of the promenade there are some of the most extensive coastal views in the North West; on a clear day Wales and the mountains of Snowdonia can be seen to the left while the Lake District mountains lie straight ahead together with the Cumbrian coastline and towns such as Barrow. Out to sea the giant oil drilling stations stand like lonely sentinels.

There are views inland as well, most notably towards the Lancashire Fells, but look down Duchess Drive, where there are three-storey flats on either side, and the communications station at Inskip will be seen. Like the fells and Blackpool Tower, the aerials at Inskip can be seen on many of the walks. As the path loses height we approach the imposing building, set well back in its own grounds, that was the Miners' Convalescent Home, completed in 1927 for the miners of Lancashire and North Staffordshire who suffered mining-related illnesses. The scale of the place reflects the importance of mining in the region at the time. As we draw level with this well-known local landmark look down towards the lower promenade where a marker indicates that it is 3000 metres to Talbot Square and 2500 metres to Anchorsholme Park. Eventually we reach, arguably, the most impressive tram stop at Bispham, more akin to a small railway station, complete with toilet facilities. Indeed, it is named Bispham Station. A choice of routes is now available. For a walk through the remnants of old Bispham and returning to Norbreck turn right at the traffic lights into Red Bank Road and follow the directions from 5.

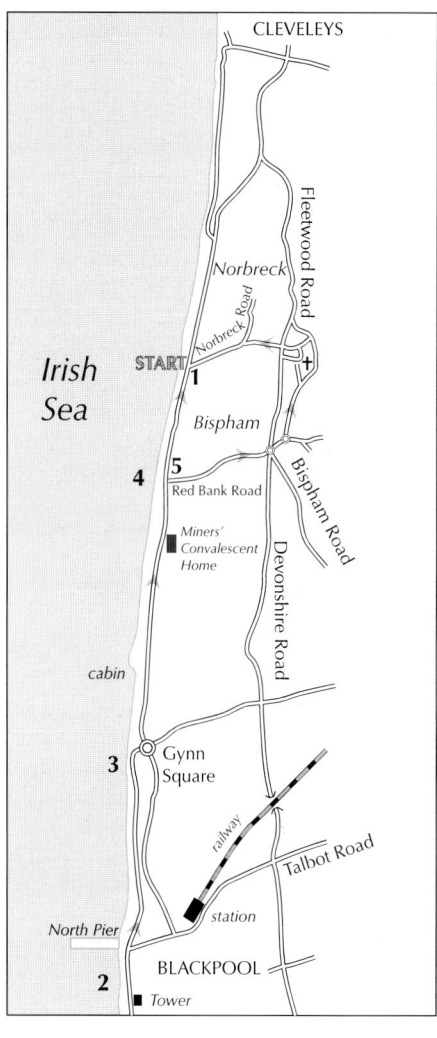

Resuming along the promenade look out for Pennystone Road, the first road on the right beyond the traffic lights. The name recalls Pennystone rock which, along with the nearer Carlin Stone rock, can still be seen at low tide. There are some who believe that they are remnants of the long lost village of Singleton Thorpe. As we make our way back to Norbreck note the attractive tram shelters in an Edwardian style with ogee roofs. Arriving back at the Norbreck Castle Hotel return to the start.

– 23 –

Fylde Coast and Country Walks

Miners' home, Bispham

5 Walk down Red Bank Road for about half a mile to the roundabout and cross straight over into Bispham village. Proceed to the next roundabout and turn left into All Hallows Road. Beyond the last shops there are some older houses, reminders of old Bispham when this road was the main route through the village. One of the houses, at an angle to the road, bears the date 1820 with a rubble boundary wall. Christmas Cottage is probably quite old too while, a little further on, there is a section of pebble walling (more familiar in Lytham) topped with concrete outside St Bernadette Roman Catholic School. Other random sections of boundary walls, composed of cobbles, can be seen along this road. They represent the few remaining reminders of this part of Bispham's long history. The tower of All Hallows Church can be seen ahead and, as we draw closer to it, note the old stone gateposts on the left just before Church Villa. They may have marked the entrance to a farm at one time. Now pass through the lychgate and into the churchyard for a closer look at the church which dates from the thirteenth century though it has been substantially rebuilt on more than one occasion. Returning to the road, proceed to where it meets All Saints Road, once the main junction in the old village. At this point it becomes Fleetwood Road with playing fields on the right. The old hedge that borders these recreation grounds almost certainly formed the boundary to agricultural fields in the distant past. Beyond the playing fields Fleetwood Road bends sharply to the left and, across the road, more cobbled walling can be seen. At the left-hand bend turn left into Guildford Avenue and follow the road to the junction with Devonshire Road. Cross over and continue along Guildford Avenue and Norbreck Road to the sea front and the start.

WALK 5

Poulton-le-Fylde

A walk around one of the oldest towns on the Fylde.

Distance:	2¾ miles
Start:	From the pay and display car park in the centre of Poulton. Grid reference: 347395.
Map:	OS Pathfinder 658/678; OS Landranger 102
Time allowed:	1½ hours
Conditions and difficulties:	Walking boots are likely to be sufficient in dry conditions but, after prolonged periods of rain and during the winter months it is advisable to wear Wellington boots
Facilities:	There are all the usual facilities of a small town including toilet facilities at the side of the car park
Public transport:	There are regular bus services

1 From the car park turn right into Ball Street to St Chad's parish church. St Chad's is largely an eighteenth- and nineteenth-century rebuilding of an earlier church for which there are records dating back to the eleventh century. The family vault of the Fleetwoods of Rossall Hall has a separate entrance on the south side. Behind the church is the Market Place, centre of the old town, where relics of

St Chad's Parish Church from the market place

– 25 –

Poulton's past can be seen. There are the stone stocks, the market cross, the fish stones, a seventeenth-century whipping post and a lamp erected in 1887 for Queen Victoria's Golden Jubilee.

Now return to Ball Street and, turning right, continue over the crossroads into Vicarage Road, passing a building on the far right-hand corner that still bears the title, 'Poulton Savings Bank'. Proceed along Vicarage Road past the recreation ground and, at the junction, turn left into Station Road. The name of this road refers to the original station at Poulton which was situated close to the junction with Breck Road. We shall encounter the site of the old station later but, for now, cross over the railway and, immediately, turn right down an alleyway leading onto Howarth Crescent. Proceed to the far end of this road where two paths will be seen ahead. Ignore the one that drops down to the right but go straight ahead, over what was once a footbridge that spanned the original railway lines through Poulton. It is difficult to visualize a railway landscape here, now that the cuttings have been filled in and occupied by housing on the right and an extension to the playing fields on the left. Pressing ahead past Hodgson High School on the right we reach Moorland Road. Turn right at this junction and then take first left into the delightful Little Poulton Lane.

2 Walking down this lane it is easy to feel a sense of leaving the modern world behind. Although there are houses of modern construction there are also older dwellings such as Mill Farm and Abbotside Cottage (with its stone mullioned windows and a date stone of 1695). Further on there is the whitewashed Old Farm bearing the date 1723. Towards the far end of the lane note the old stone gate posts outside Little Poulton Hall before reaching a stile at the lane end leading onto a broad, grassy track. There is, initially, a ditch on the right and, further on, the track opens out into a field. Follow the right-hand edge until reaching Main Dyke, which falls gradually away from Marton Mere to the river Wyre at Skippool. The path turns left with this meandering watercourse to reach a stile, from which point it becomes more enclosed. Soon we encounter a residential area and a caravan site on our left, a contrast with the fields on the other side of the dyke.

3 At the main road turn left, following Breck Road past the River Wyre hotel and left again at the roundabout. Now look out at once for a small entrance on the right, just beyond the pillar box as our route along a public footpath now resumes, leading to a footbridge. Across the bridge we now follow the stream to the left until reaching another footbridge in a hedge. Cross over the ditch and turn right along a narrow grassy path. Care is required because of the barbed wire fence on our left. The next footbridge leads us onto a golf course. Follow the path to the right and then proceed in the same direction as before, across three fairways, taking care to avoid stray golf balls. There are plenty of signs pointing straight ahead but half way across the course, at a fingerpost, turn left. As we turn, a ditch will be seen and we should keep to the left of it, alongside a hedge, before veering left to a footbridge. Once over the bridge aim for the far right corner of the course, making sure to keep to the right of the club house. A gap in the hedge leads us out to the edge of playing fields. Turn left and follow the narrow enclosed path which passes Moorland Tennis Club on the left and what was a former railway goods yard on the right until redeveloped. It was in this vicinity where

Walk 5: Poulton-le-Fylde

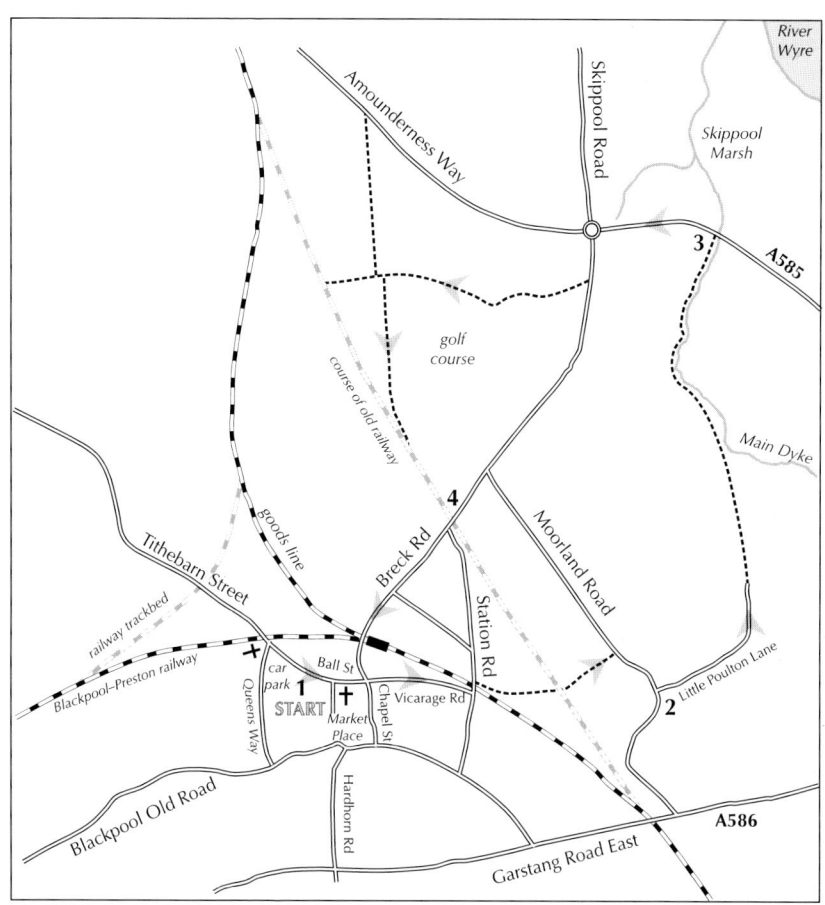

a train from Blackpool left the track as it took the sharp curve to the old station at too great a speed. Three people were killed and sixteen injured as a result of that accident in 1893 that led to the present alignment of the railway through the town.

4 Soon the path emerges onto Breck Road, once again, beside the entrance to the tennis club. Turn right but, as we approach the traffic lights, look to the left as this was the site of the old station at Poulton. Note the Royal Oak Hotel on the corner which was used as a makeshift hospital after the accident. Beyond the traffic lights on the right is the Wyre Borough Council Civic Centre housing the council's offices. We continue along Breck Road, lined with pleasant, semi-detached villas. Towards the top of the road we reach the present station, noted for its long platforms. If able to look over the bridge on the right one can see the junction with the sparsely used Fleetwood line diverging to the right from the main line to Blackpool. On reaching the crossroads at the top of the hill turn right to return, past the church, to the car park.

WALK 6

Marton and Blackpool

A surprisingly pleasant and alternative way of visiting the centre of Blackpool with the added benefit of no parking charges. Not recommended for your week's shopping!

Distance:	2½, 5¼ or 7¼ miles
Start:	Park near the field entrance on Lawson Road at the junction with Lancaster Road. Grid reference: 334352
Map:	OS Pathfinder 678; A-Z Blackpool; OS Landranger 102
Time allowed:	1½ (a leisurely stroll around the mere), 2½ (round trip to Blackpool from Marton) or 3½ hours (Blackpool and the mere).
Conditions and difficulties:	Normal shoes will be sufficient except around Marton Mere in damp conditions when walking boots are advisable
Facilities:	The usual range of facilities associated with a town the size of Blackpool. Don't forget a pair of binoculars if walking around Marton Mere
Public transport:	There is a regular bus service from Blackpool

1 From the road drop down to the playing field but, as we pass through the gateway, look ahead and a little to the right for a view of Staining Mill on the horizon. It is a private residence now and one of just four windmills on the Fylde that retains its sails. Cross the field to reach the embankment on the far side. A formal path will be found on the top of the embankment where, if the walk is to be restricted to the Marton Mere option only, turn right and follow the directions under section 5. Otherwise, turn left initially but, at a junction, turn right along a path towards the hotel complex. Almost immediately after a right-hand corner turn first left towards the hotel and turn left again at the next junction to reach, eventually, the drive to the hotel. Incidentally, if you hear any exotic animal sounds, don't be surprised as Blackpool Zoo is just beyond the hotel complex. Turn left down the drive to reach the busy main road but remember, if you have not been able to follow the directions from the embankment for any reason, just aim to the left of the hotel and the drive to the main road will be found.

Across the other side of the road is Stanley Park. Cross over from the drive to locate a path, just to the left, leading into the park. Take the path straight ahead, passing the lake on the right; ignore paths to the right and to the left but, where two paths branch off right, ignore the path leading down to the lake but take the next path to pass the bandstand and the amphitheatre on the right. Continue over a crossroad of paths to reach the Italian Gardens. Follow the path round to the left but note that our exit will be opposite our entry point. These gardens are impressively contained by a screen with Roman-like Doric pillars around the circumference while a lake and fountain form the centrepiece. There are some well-designed vistas from here, especially to the left along a path that leads towards the Floral Clock. Having passed through the gardens continue until

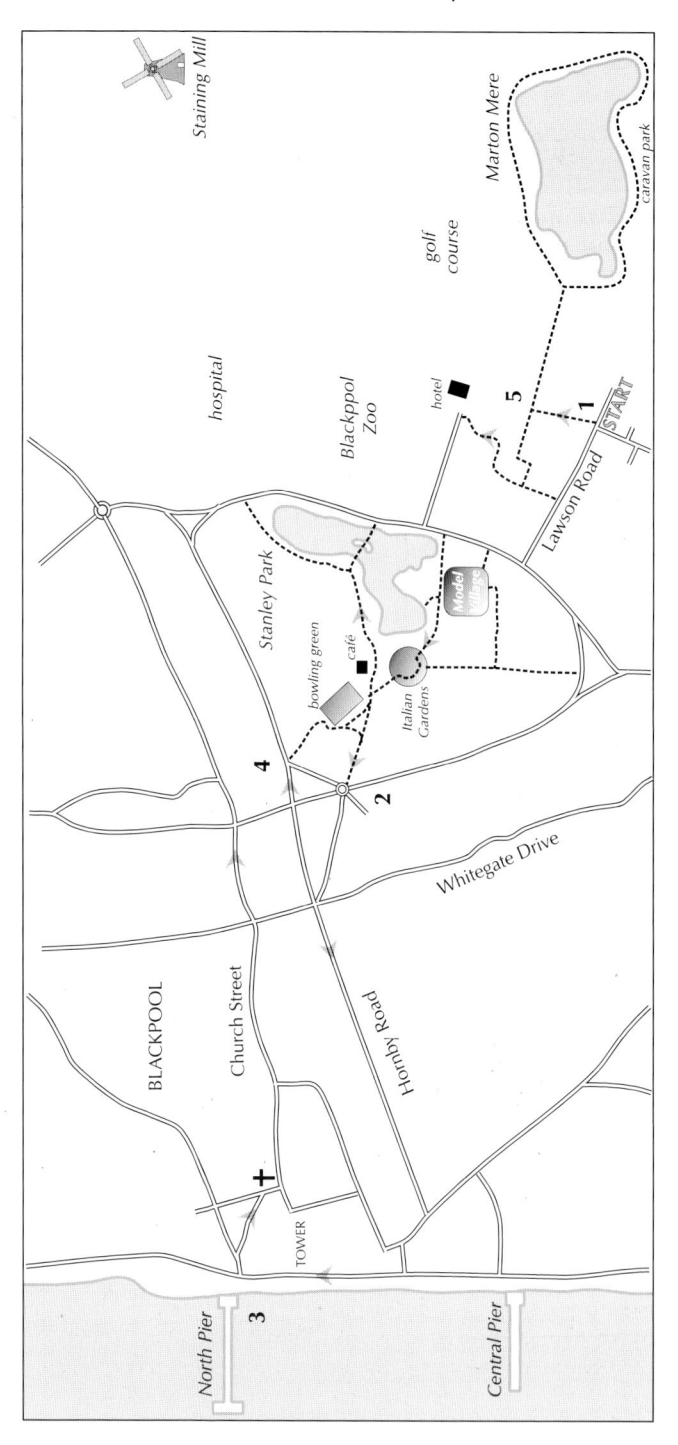

Walk 6: Marton and Blackpool

Fylde Coast and Country Walks

Floral Clock, Stanley Park

Walk 6: Marton and Blackpool

reaching Mawson Drive, one of the main vehicular drives into the park. Turn left to leave Stanley Park at impressive gates.

2 Cross over the roundabout and proceed down Mere Road, directly opposite the park gates. At the traffic lights with Whitegate Drive cross straight over and continue in the same direction along Hornby Road. For those of you who thought Blackpool was flat the gradient up to the brow on this road should come as something of a surprise but, in fact, there are several instances of even steeper gradients around the town. Before reaching the next traffic lights look out for another view of the tower ahead and to the right. Having crossed Park Road we continue along Hornby Road to more traffic lights and, by now, the Sea Life Centre on the promenade is visible. At the T-junction with Central Drive a large car park will be seen ahead; this is the site of the former Blackpool Central station which closed in 1964. Turn right here and then first left. On the left are the very generous toilet facilities that were once situated off the station's concourse and testimony to the size of this terminus and the number of passengers it handled. The sea is just ahead and, at the traffic lights, we turn right onto the Golden Mile with its famous trams and amusements, including Tower World on our right which gives access to Blackpool Tower, opened in 1894 as an imitation of Eiffel Tower. At 518 feet (158 metres) it was the tallest building in the country when built. Keep on to the traffic lights at North Pier, the oldest and longest of the three piers.

3 Our way back from the pier is by heading directly inland from the sea into Talbot Square (where there are further toilet facilities) and then along the right fork, Clifton Street, to Abingdon Street. Turn right to come face to face with the winter Gardens which is worth a quick look round at the very least. As we walk away from the town centre note the parish church, St John the Evangelist, on the left. Continue to a junction and take the right fork along Church Street, noted for its solicitors, accountants and estate agents. Carry on straight down this road ignoring Park Road that bends to the right. At the traffic lights cross over and pass the No3, once a staging inn. Now walk up Newton Drive to the first traffic lights and turn right into Beech Avenue and then left at the next traffic lights into Forest Gate. Keep along this road until Stanley Park is reached. An entrance will be found just beyond the road junction on the right.

4 Enter the park and take the main path straight down. In the summer it is worth a small diversion to the right to pass through the Rose Garden before rejoining the main path via the first exit left from the garden. Continue ahead until a viewing area is reached that overlooks the bowling green. Turn right, down the steps to the bowling green and turn right again to return to the park. Now take the left fork in the junction of paths and down to Mawson Drive once again. The cricket ground stands ahead of us; it occasionally plays host to county cricket matches. Turn left along the drive to reach a junction of paths. The right-hand path leads back to the Italian Gardens but we need to take the centre path leading to the imposing Art Deco cafe of 1936. There is a fine view from here towards the Italian Gardens and, beyond, to the Floral Clock. If not wishing to stop for refreshments continue towards the lake but, without going down to the lakeside,

Fylde Coast and Country Walks

take the left-hand path behind the park buildings. Ignore the first two paths on the right beyond the buildings but, at the third, take the right fork towards the bridge over the lake. Cross the balustraded bridge to an island in the lake and then across another similar bridge to the far side of the lake and out of the park onto the main road at a point virtually opposite the zoo.

Turn right and, at a convenient spot, cross the road and turn first left up the drive towards the hotel. Pass the side of a small lake and take the first path on the right. Continue round the outside of the hotel's boundary fence and take the first right turn again. This path soon joins a broad track from the left and then, a few yards further on, it makes a sharp left-hand turn as it heads towards a road. We then need to take the next path on the left leading towards Marton Mere. If returning to the car turn right on reaching the playing fields; otherwise follow the instructions under section 5.

5 Proceed along the path which, in time, merges with a broader track. The tower-like building that can be seen ahead is the Premium Bonds office block. The wide track eventually reaches a junction of tracks before the boundary of Marton Mere and our route is ahead and through the gap to the right of a gate. Take the right-hand path within the boundary of the reserve which was designated a Site of Special Scientific Interest by the Nature Conservancy Council in 1979 and a Local Nature Reserve by Blackpool Borough Council in 1991. The mere has a particularly close link with Blackpool in that it was its peaty waters draining into the sea that gave rise to the name Black Poole. It was once much larger and evidence of its former banks can be seen in places as can the clues to a former use of the surrounding land as a refuse tip (until 1972), especially in winter. As we continue along this path look out for the Warden's Office on the right which, because of the warden's various duties, is open at irregular times. Access to the office is via a gate and, when in residence, the warden is very helpful. There are various hides that have been established around the site and an access path on the left leads to the first of these. Returning to the main path we soon encounter a gate that leads us onto a more open area.

We now need to follow the path round to the left, between the caravan site and the lake. At this point it is worth mentioning something about the birds that can be seen. To start with, if you know little about birds and would like to know more, a simple introductory book on bird identification would be useful. It may also be helpful, in the absence of the warden, to chat to someone who looks as if they may know something about birds (someone carrying binoculars would be a good bet). Bird watchers are often a very helpful group of enthusiasts. As it is free to walk around the lake, Marton Mere is a very useful place to begin bird watching as a hobby because of the variety of birds including those of the sea, freshwater, farmland, woodland and reeds. May and June are particularly interesting times to visit as the tree foliage is not yet too dense and the local bird population is swelled by the summer visitors including the different species of warblers that can be seen among the trees and reeds. The writer has personally seen in excess of forty species of birds on one visit and, in time, a considerable number will be spotted including the occasional rarity such as a bittern or marsh harrier.

Continue to the far end of the lake, making use of the hides which may contain

Walk 6: Marton and Blackpool

A Blackpool tram on the promenade. Blackpool Tower is in the background

bird-identification posters. Follow the path round to the left at the far end and cross a metal bridge over the escape waters that eventually find a way to the river Wyre at Skippool and the Ribble estuary at Lytham. Returning around the other side of the lake we should now be able to see Blackpool Tower ahead and Marton windmill to the left (left of the Premium Bonds office). This windmill was built in 1838 and last worked in the 1920s. Eventually we reach the gate leading out of the reserve and onto the broad track that stretches straight ahead. On reaching the playing fields look out for a suitable path off the embankment and then return across the field to the start.

WALK 7

Singleton

Blackpool Tower to the west and the Lancashire fells on the eastern boundary of this region are often in view from this walk, as are three of the Fylde's windmills.

Distance:	9 miles
Start:	From the centre of Singleton at the quaint former fire station, take Church Road and park by Singleton Church. Grid reference: 385384
Maps:	OS Pathfinder 678; OS Landranger 102
Time allowed:	4½ hours. Walkers using public transport should ideally allow over 5 hours
Conditions and difficulties:	Walking boots should be sufficient in dry conditions but Wellington boots are advisable after prolonged periods of rain. Care is needed when crossing the railway
Facilities:	Eagle and Child, Weeton, and Great Singleton Post Office at the junction of Station Road and Lodge Lane in the centre of the village
Public transport:	There is a bus service from Blackpool and Preston

1 Much of Singleton village was built with the money of rich cotton manufacturer, Thomas Miller, who lived in Singleton Hall. The gate on the opposite side of the road from the church entrance was once used regularly by the Miller family as it gave pedestrian access from the hall to the church. Now enter the churchyard of St Anne and, well to the left of the lychgate, is the Miller family vault. Walk round to the left to locate a gate in the wall. This leads on to a narrow path between hawthorn hedges and takes us directly to the B5269 road. Along the way Blackpool Tower is visible to the right and the Lancashire fells and hills are in the distance to our left. Beyond the kissing gate at the far end turn left along the pavement but only briefly as we cross the road taking the first right up the concrete drive to Brackenscales Farm. The drive passes straight through the farm, in between the buildings ahead (avoid turning right into the farmyard), and then maintaining the same direction. Beyond the farm the concrete drive continues to a gate at which point it becomes a track.

To reach the stile ahead we must now leave the track, turning through the gate on the right and resuming the previous direction along the left-hand boundary of the field. Cross the stile at the far end and continue as before to pass alongside Moss House. Just beyond the house take the gate on the right and turn left along the grassy track reaching a stile beside a gate. At this point turn left walking next to the hedge to cross another stile by gates and then proceed across the footbridge, over a ditch, which is now alongside us as we turn right into the next field as far as the corner. Here, a left turn, with the hedge now on our right, leads to another field corner and a stile. Turn right here next to a ditch. The ground can

– 34 –

Walk 7: Singleton

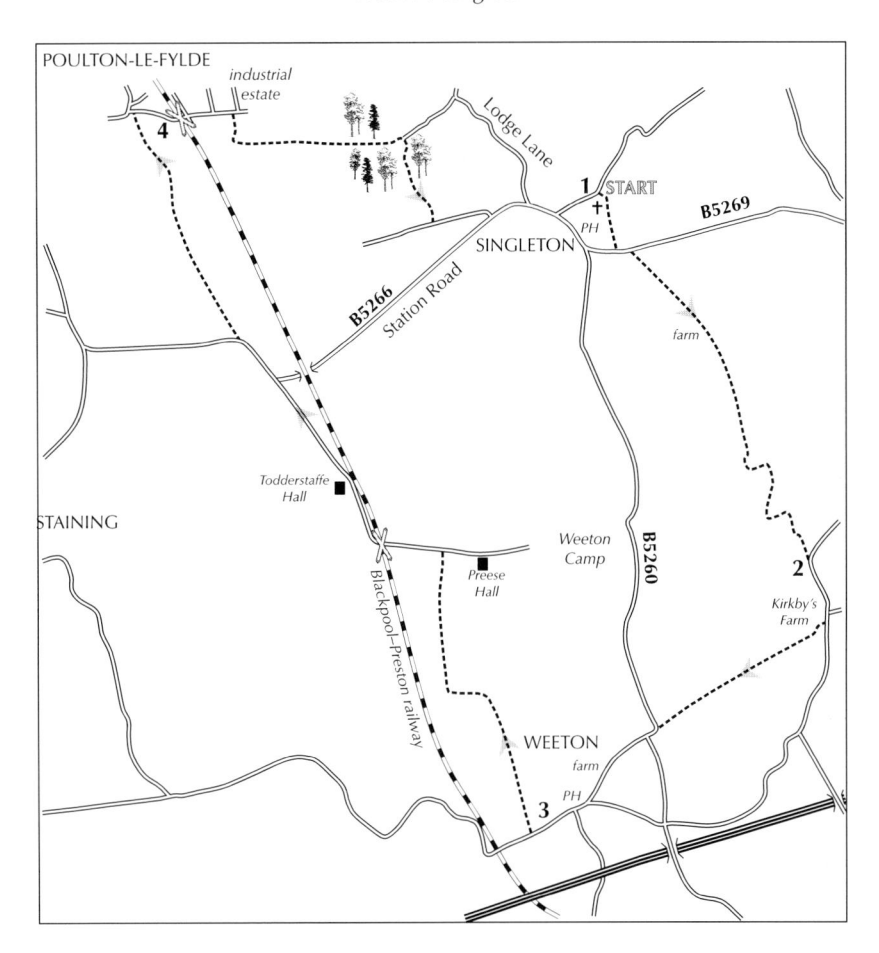

be a little water-logged in this vicinity but soon a gate is reached at the bend of a quiet lane allowing quicker progress to be made.

2. Turn right down the lane, eventually passing a fishing lake on the left, before reaching a junction. Ignore the road to the left leading to the hamlet of Greenhalgh but continue a little further to the driveway at Kirby's Farm. Turn, as waymarked, into the drive and forecourt keeping left onto a stony track as far as a stile that brings us to a narrow pasture. The way is forward alongside the hedge and shortly the pasture opens up before reaching a small gate. Walking through the next field Singleton church spire can be glimpsed to the right and, passing through a gateway, Blackpool Tower reappears in the distance. Indeed, the bulbous top of the National Savings offices, the edge of the huge roller coaster known as 'The Big One' and even Marton windmill can be discerned on the horizon when weather conditions permit. Continue through a series of gateways to a crest and from here it is a short distance to the stile leading us out onto the road at a sharp bend. Fortunately, there is a pavement leading directly forward to Weeton village.

Fylde Coast and Country Walks

On the way, Weeton Road on the left is passed and, further on, a farm before reaching the triangular green and the Eagle and Child pub. The public house is quite deceiving as it actually dates back to the sixteenth century and takes its name from the family crest of the Earls of Derby. Originally thatched, the roof was replaced in the 1960s following a fire.

3 Continue in the same direction to the far end of the village to where the pavement ends. Caution is required but only briefly as, passing the village boundary, the brow of the hill is reached and a sign directs us along a track to the right where a house with a grand two-storey pillared entrance is encountered. Over a stile and along this ridge there are unimpeded views towards Blackpool. Marton windmill is now clearly seen in front of the Pleasure Beach and Staining Mill, to the north of Blackpool Tower, while the main railway line to Blackpool is in the foreground on our left. Here was the scene of the worst railway accident on the Fylde when a diesel train ran into the back of a stationary ballast train in July 1961, killing seven people and injuring 116. Keep in a straight line as the path drops down to a footbridge over a ditch. The sheds of Weeton Army Barracks can be seen on the right before reaching the bridge where, having crossed it, turn left alongside the ditch. Beyond the second stile turn right with a hedge and keep in the same direction, passing a small wood, to draw level with the red brick Preece Hall on the right. The path here becomes a track and runs along the edge of the next field to meet a more prominent track beyond a stile. Turn left here and head straight for the railway. Having crossed Main Dyke and passed Crossings Wood the level crossing is reached with Blackpool Tower straight ahead. There is a clear view down the line for over a mile to our left **but, on the right, trains can appear almost without warning so great care should be taken when crossing and children should be firmly guided across.** Milepost 12 will be noticed by the track on the right indicating 12 miles from Preston.

Now turn right up the track towards Todderstaffe Hall, passing its drive on the left and a public footpath a little further on. The track now becomes a made-up lane dropping down towards the B5266. The railway re-appears from the cutting and Staining windmill (which could be glimpsed earlier) is clearly visible on the left complete with sails. The busy road ahead is joined at a sharp bend. Unfortunately, there is no pavement along this section but, thankfully, it is short with our exit being visible ahead at the next bend. Here the road turns sharply to the left while our way continues up the enclosed track keeping left of the farm buildings. The track ends at a stile, to the left of a gate, and we must now pursue a straight course across the field to a crest. There are good views along this section towards the fells and Singleton church spire can be seen, once again, in the trees. We reach the highest point on the walk at the next stile from which a new vista opens up to the north with Poulton-le-Fylde in the foreground, the tower of its parish church prominent. The Lake District mountains can be seen in the distance on a clear day while, looking over to the left, the water tower north of Blackpool will be seen and it is also possible to see Rossall School further north on the horizon. Look out, too, for the windmills as it is possible to see three. Marsh Mill may be seen beyond Poulton while Marton Mill is in the opposite direction looking back to the left. Looking in a direction south of the Pleasure Beach it is also possible in winter to pick out Staining Mill, partially

Walk 7: Singleton

The old fire station at Singleton

hidden by trees. Who knows, maybe this is the only place in Britain from where three windmills with sails can be seen.

Crossing the stile here go forward with the hedge to the right. At a stile continue into the next field ignoring the gate on the right. A track now makes its way to the left-hand corner of the field but, instead, keep ahead, veering half-left only on approaching the fence ahead to locate a stile in the hedge below. Having crossed now proceed slightly left to reach a footbridge. This crosses a ditch to give access to a footpath leading to Holts Lane. The path ends in a field but, making a way between the houses ahead, a gate will be found to arrive at the lane which is, in fact, a quiet residential cul-de-sac. Turn right to reach the railway at a crossing.

4 Taking care to cross the railway continue ahead along a path that leads us onto Poulton Industrial Estate at a junction. Go straight ahead to eventually pass Cocker Avenue on the left and, just before reaching the next junction with Beacon Road on the left, turn right down a concrete roadway as indicated by the public footpath sign. Although this is a commercial yard proceed ahead, with a fence on our left, and through the gap in the corner. At first glance our way appears to be blocked by a fence ahead but panels are missing to allow access through a yard (waymark signs should be visible on the fence posts). It may be necessary to pick one's way around parked vehicles in the yard but don't be put off and, at the far end on the right, a further gap allows us to pass through the fence and turn left to reach a footbridge. This crosses Main Dyke which forms the southern boundary of the industrial estate. Returning to the open countryside our immediate route is straightforward as the path rises up the right-hand side to the far corner

of the field. Here, continue in the same direction on an enclosed path reaching woodland. A large pool on the right will be seen followed by a smaller pool and, shortly before the wood ends, look for a gate on the right. This is our access into a field which we skirt along its left-hand boundary just outside Knowle Wood on our left. Cross over a stile and, once beyond the end of the wood, veer to the left edge of the field to vacate it at a hurdle stile. This brings us onto Carr Lane where we turn left, passing Mount Farm on the edge of Singleton.

Emerging on to a busy road turn left at the village boundary and, using a pavement, walk along the curiously named Station Road to the junction at the centre of the village. There was, indeed, a station called Singleton long ago but according to one established railway book the station was not at the point where the road meets the railway but south of milepost 12, encountered earlier at the level crossing near Todderstaffe Hall! At the junction turn right along Lodge Lane and continue to the next junction where the minute black-and-white design of fire station is now an electricity sub station. Turn left up Church Road to the starting point.

WALK 8

Weeton and Greenhalgh

A walk through undulating farmland in one of the highest areas of the Fylde (about 30 metres) crossing its two principal transport arteries, the M55 motorway and the main railway line to Blackpool.

Distance:	5¼ miles
Start:	From the Eagle and Child in the centre of Weeton. Grid reference: 385347
Maps:	OS Pathfinder 678 and 679; OS Landranger 102
Time allowed:	2½ hours
Conditions and difficulties:	Walking boots should be sufficient except after periods of prolonged rain when Wellington boots would be preferable. Care is needed when crossing the railway
Facilities:	The Eagle and Child is situated in the centre of Weeton. There is also a payphone opposite the village green
Public transport:	There is a bus service between Blackpool and Preston

1 If emerging from the Eagle and Child head left, taking the left fork at the village green. Beyond the farm on our left we leave the village and emerge into open countryside. Although the B5260 can be quite a busy road we have the benefit of a pavement until leaving the road at a sharp left-hand bend. Before then look back to the left for a view of Blackpool Tower.

Shortly after passing the junction with Weeton Road on our right look for a convenient point to cross and take the stile on the right at the sharp left-hand bend and enter a field. Now follow a straight course ahead keeping the hedge to our right and pass through a series of gateways and along the edges of five fields. On entering the fifth field look left for a glimpse of the spire of Singleton church. Leaving this field at a small gate we emerge into a pasture that narrows towards a stile. Once over this we follow the same direction along a track that passes Kirby's Farm and Shorrocks Barn on our left before arriving at a quiet lane.

2 Turn left and then first right into Greenhalgh Lane, shortly entering the hamlet of Greenhalgh. Passing the post box, set in a wall on our left, we should now see the public footpath sign on our right signifying a change of direction. The sign is opposite South View Farm and we now turn right down the path through a series of gates into a field with a hedge immediately on our left. Half way along the field a pond is encountered to the right and, where the hedge comes to an end, continue ahead to a footbridge and a stile in the hedge. Now look straight ahead for another stile at the nearest point in the hedge opposite. Once over that stile turn left for about 50 yards, alongside the field boundary, to a track running through the middle of the field. With a gate on our left we now turn right along the track up the field, passing a large hollow on the right, until

Fylde Coast and Country Walks

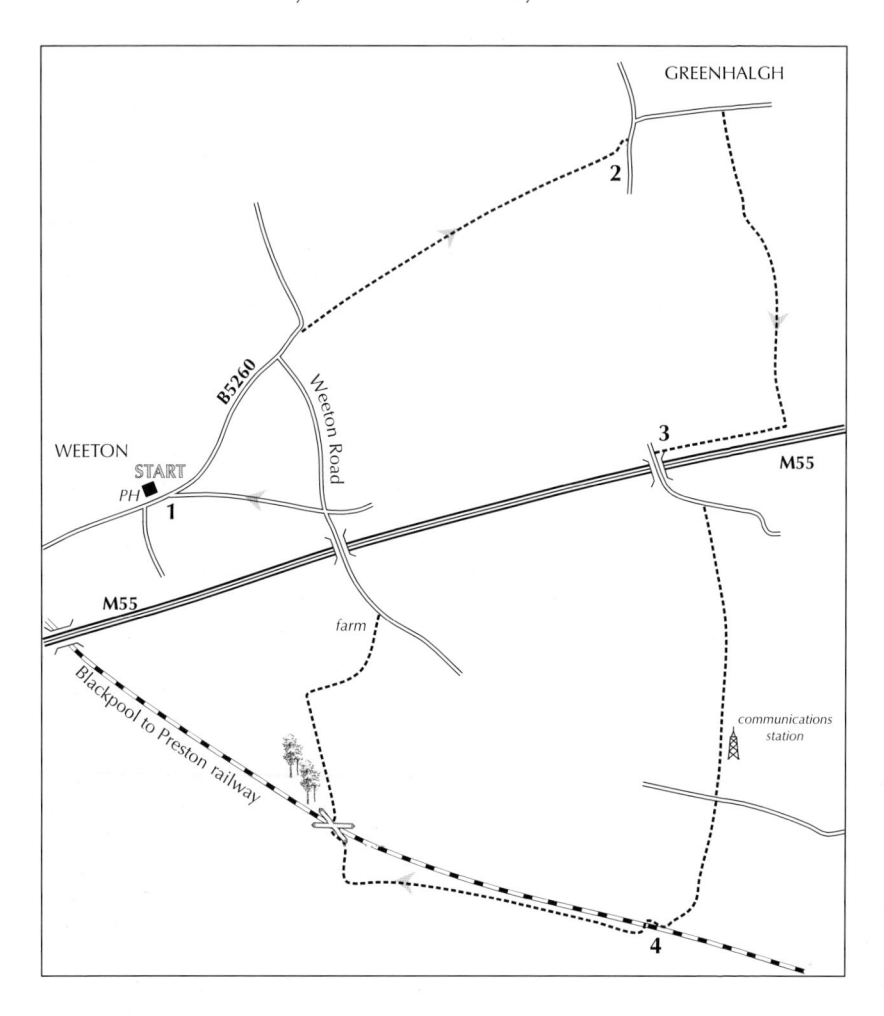

reaching a boundary of hedges and trees. Carry on straight ahead through the next field and over the brow, dropping down to a stile ahead and, once again, walk up to the crest of the next field in the same direction to arrive at the fence beside the M55 motorway. Now turn right alongside the fence, crossing a stile next to a gate in the field corner where a paved track is joined.

3 Where the track meets a lane turn left at the junction to cross the motorway. Just at the point where the pavement ends and before reaching the first house turn right over a stile by a gate. Our direction is straight ahead towards the radio mast, passing a pond on the right and crossing a footbridge over a ditch. From the footbridge we now need to go straight ahead to reach a gate on the other side of the field. Walking up the next field towards the aerials look left for a distant view of the Lancashire fells and, as we pass by the side of the Civil

Walk 8: Weeton and Greenhalgh

Aviation Authority's radio station on our left, we join its track leading out of the field via a stile.

Now cross the road to another stile. Ahead is the Preston to Blackpool railway line and, beyond, in the distance, the spire of Wrea Green church. Take the track from the stile down towards the railway. As the fence on our left turns away at right angles go forward, a little to the right, to locate a stile in the fence. Crossing the footbridge it is just a few yards to the railway where a stile will be found guiding us to the right and along the path, between the field's boundary fence and the railway, to reach a footbridge. Care is required here as, in my experience, it is easy to be tripped up by the long sprawling branches of brambles and other plants.

4 Take the footbridge over the railway and, as we drop down to the other side, look into the field ahead. There are signs of previous uses here and, indeed, there was a brickworks at one time that supplied much local brick. There was also a branch line from Wrea Green curving in towards the Blackpool line that provided a connection between Lytham and Blackpool before the coast line was connected at Lytham. Now turn right onto the track alongside and above the line. Once again, watch out for spreading branches, especially those with thorns! Keep with this track that rises to a crest before dropping down to reach a bridge spanning the railway. Our way forward is via steps down, passing under the bridge (which is, in fact, an aqueduct) and up the steps on the other side to a stile. Here, turn right into a field and then through another field before reaching a stile. From here go forward, ignoring the stile on the left, until reaching steps that drop down to the railway. To save time lingering on the line it is worth noting the point at which we should climb out of the cutting but, in actual fact, there are footboards across and the way should be quite clear. The cutting may seem wide at this point and this is because there was a junction here with the direct lines through to Blackpool Central diverging to the left. Most traces of its former route, however, have disappeared. Please exercise extreme care in crossing the main line and, in particular, look to the left where a bend in the track can cause trains to appear without warning. Climb the steps up the other side and, at the top, take the stile that leads into a small field where we drop down beside the wood to a footbridge leading into the next field. Now there is a surprisingly steep climb up the right-hand side of this field alongside the hedge. The climb is brief and soon we reach another stile in the far right-hand corner of the field. Turn right again towards the farm, with the hedge on our right, and on approaching the farm boundary veer to the left, towards the house, locating a stile to its right (and left of a gate), leading us briefly into the farmyard. Turn immediately left down the farm drive and out onto the road.

Turn left towards the M55 which we cross and from where there are views of Blackpool Tower and the Bonds office, where the premium bonds are processed. The pavement carries on to the crossroads where we turn left into Kirkham Road. On the right is Back Lane which used to be named Mill Lane. Had we turned right at the crossroads we would have seen the foundations of the old mill at the brow of the hill. It was demolished in 1960. Soon we arrive back at Weeton, one of several estate villages once under the control of the Earls of Derby. The name of the inn, Eagle and Child, is in fact taken from their coat of arms. It is

The Eagle and Child at Weeton

one of the Fylde's oldest licenced premises and is believed to have held its licence since 1585 although the building has been much altered since then. It is also said that Oliver Cromwell spent a night here during the Civil War. More recently it was targeted for bombing by the IRA due to its popularity with soldiers from the Weeton army camp nearby. Note the mounting steps for horse riders and the column, inscribed 1755. It is also worth noting the thatched house on the left-hand side as we draw level with the green. It is believed to date from 1677.

WALK 9

Lytham

A town walk of contrasts featuring views across the estuary, a tree-lined avenue and the attractive shopping centre.

Distance:	3¼ miles
Start:	From the windmill on Lytham green. Grid reference: 371270
Maps:	OS Pathfinder 678; OS Landranger 102
Time allowed:	About 1½ hours
Conditions and difficulties:	Normal shoes are likely to be sufficient for most occasions but it is wise to bring extra clothing as, under windy conditions, the wind chill factor can be more pronounced by the side of the estuary
Facilities:	There is an excellent variety of cafes, restaurants and pubs in the town centre. Some of the cafes have tables outside in the summer. There are also several shops offering sandwiches and cakes. Public toilets are situated adjacent to the windmill and there are public telephones and a tourist information centre along the route as it passes through the town
Public transport:	There is a regular bus and train service to Lytham from both Blackpool and Preston

1 With our back to the windmill and facing the estuary turn left with the Ribble on our right. There are extensive views across the river to Southport and Winter Hill, identifiable by its television mast. On clear days it is even possible to see

The windmill and old lifeboat station on Lytham Green

Fylde Coast and Country Walks

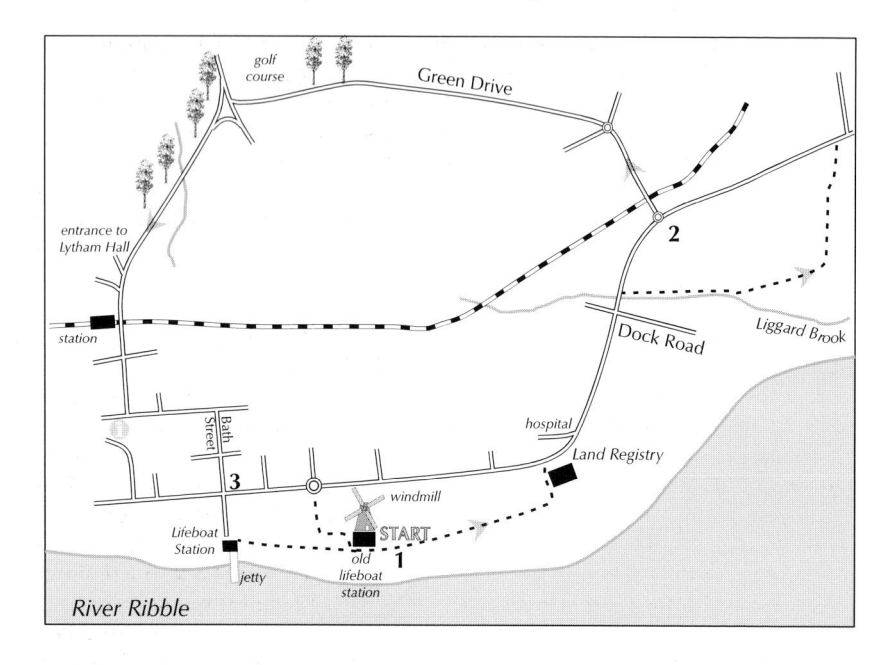

the North Wales coastline further round to the right. The coastal path ends at the boundary of the Land Registry forcing us inland to the main road, where we turn right and pass the Land Registry (once the site of the former Customs House) and Lytham Hospital to our left. The hospital was built in 1871 and funded by the Squire of Lytham, Colonel John Talbot Clifton. Continue through the traffic lights at the junction with Dock Road. The name of the road is a reminder of the shipbuilding industry that had a presence here for over a hundred years. During the most active period nearly a thousand ships were built, mainly of the smaller variety such as tugs and ferries. A considerable amount of trade was conducted with African and South American countries and, for many years, it was believed that the boat known as the *African Queen,* which featured in the film of the same name, was built here. The truth appears to be that it shared its duties on Lake Albert in Africa with a boat built in Lytham and while many similar boats were built here they did not include that which gave its name to the film. The former shipbuilding site, which closed in 1955, is now occupied by an industrial estate though modern housing development encroaches ever closer.

Continue now a little further to Graving Dock Bridge which crosses Liggard Brook and, at the far side of the bridge, turn right up the steps onto the embankment, as indicated by the public footpath sign. If wishing to cut short this walk go straight ahead along the main road to the mini roundabout and turn left there to join us again at 2. Otherwise proceed along the embankment and note the tidal brook down to the right, usually host to a variety of smaller boats of varying sizes and condition. The grassy path soon splits at which point we follow the path to the left, close to the boundary fence separating us from more industrial units. Passing allotments on the right we reach a left-hand corner. Continue along

Walk 9: Lytham

the grassy path until it slopes down to join the boat yard of Ribble Cruising Club. Proceed to the left of the yard to reach the main road opposite the car showroom. There was once a railway connection into the docks from the main line to Lytham. It followed a course roughly in line with the side road to the right of the car dealers. This access road leads to another industrial estate and, just behind, lies the railway where, in 1924, one of the worst railway accidents on the Fylde occurred. A Liverpool-Blackpool express left the rails at this point and ploughed into the signal box. Twelve people died and thirty-five were injured. Now turn left as far as the mini roundabout.

2 At the roundabout turn right into Saltcotes Road and over the bridge spanning the branch line to Lytham and Blackpool South. The line is a basic single track whereas once it was double track and boasted a service to London. Opened in 1846 the railway's original terminus was at Station Road in Lytham (the site is now occupied by the fire station) and it was not until 1874, after the old Preston and Wyre Railway had been acquired jointly by the Lancashire and Yorkshire Railway and the London and North Western Railway, that a through route was provided to Blackpool. At the next mini roundabout look out for the sign for Green Drive, at the far side of the junction. As we enter this attractive tree-lined, car-free (except for access) thoroughfare, note Swiss Lodge on the right. Built in 1884 in memory of Thomas Henry Clifton MP this was once part of the Clifton family estate, as was Green Drive, given to the town by John Talbot Clifton in 1925 to celebrate the Golden Jubilee of the founding of St Annes. Along this stretch a variety of the more common woodland birds can be seen including warblers in summer and grey squirrels are often present.

At the junction of roads at the other end of Green Drive cross to the far pavement on Ballam Road and go left alongside the boundary wall of Lytham Hall, passing school playing fields on our left. Note the use of sea pebbles in much of the boundary wall. This is a common feature of many walls in the town centre. Lytham Hall stands on the site of a Benedictine Priory. Some time after the dissolution of the monasteries, carried out by Henry V111, the lands were acquired by Cuthbert Clifton of Westby and in about 1610 the first hall was built. Following a serious fire the property was substantially rebuilt as an attractive Georgian mansion in 1764 to the design of John Carr of York. The last of the Clifton family to regularly reside at Lytham Hall was Mrs Violet Clifton, who died in 1961, thus outliving her husband John Talbot Clifton by thirty three years. The hall, where *Brideshead Revisited* was partly written while Evelyn Waugh was staying with his friend Henry Clifton, was later aquired by the Guardian Royal Exchange Group but is now owned by Lytham Town Trust. As the boundary wall turns in to the right continue along the main road, across the entrance to Lytham Hall (open on a number of occasions each year), and aim for the bridge that returns us over the railway, adjacent to Lytham station on the right that replaced the original terminus, and towards the shops.

Beyond the bridge look out for the memorial fountain originally erected in the Market Place for Lady Cecily Clifton, following the death of her husband in 1882. A little further on, beyond Upper Westby Street, we pass the impressive frontage of Park Street Methodist Chapel, formerly the Wesleyan Chapel built in 1868. Its powerful Corinthian columns make a bold statement so close to the town centre

Fylde Coast and Country Walks

and must have made a big impression on the local population at the time it was built. On reaching the centre of the town at Clifton Square we need to turn left but note Stringers, one of Lytham's best known shops, on the right. Originally founded in 1857 it changed its name to Stringers in 1898. Walking down Clifton Street the Ship and Royal public house will be seen on the left, by no means the first hotel to be built in Lytham but certainly one of the oldest in its present position. We now need to cross over to the far pavement and the pedestrian crossing is the ideal place. Once on the other side continue down Clifton Street to Bath Street, the next turning on the right. Bath Street is apparently so-called because bathing vans were in use from the boarding houses here when sea-bathing became fashionable from about 1820. As we walk down this street note the decorative pebble pavements featuring a variety of pictures including a windmill and a sailing boat.

3 At the far end of Bath Street we arrive at Central Beach. On the right is the Queen's Hotel, originally called the Neptune. Cross over on to the green and aim for the windmill. The green was laid out in the late eighteenth century to protect the town from a repetition of the widespread destruction caused by an exceptionally high tide in 1720. The windmill is one of the most familiar sites on the Fylde. Having returned to our starting point it is worth taking a closer look at both the windmill and the old lifeboat station. This tower mill was built in 1805, at a time when such structures replaced earlier post mills, and appeared to weather the threat brought about by steam power. However, fire damage brought about its premature end in 1919, only a few years before electrical power became widely available during the inter-war period. Since then it has had varied uses including that of a cafe but, more recently, it has become an exhibition centre showing the history of the mill and of breadmaking.

The adjacent former lifeboat station was built in 1851, mainly of sea cobbles, and funded by Colonel John Talbot Clifton. The building was taken over by the Royal National Lifeboat Institution in 1854 and remained in use until 1960 when the present station was opened just along the promenade by the jetty. One of the oldest lifeboat houses in existence it is now a permanent museum and a sad reminder of the greatest tragedy in the history of the Lifeboat Service. On 10 December 1886 the entire crew of the *Laura Janet* and Southport's *Eliza Fearnley* perished in attempting to rescue the German barque *Mexico*. Twenty seven brave lives were lost but their successful attempt to save all the stricken crew of the German boat sums up the supreme courage of these volunteers.

WALK 10

Around Wrea Green

A variety of walks from one of Lancashire's best-known villages and home to the biggest green in the county.

Distance:	From 3¾ to 7 miles
Start:	From the centre of the village beside the green on the far side from the church. Grid reference: 396314
Map:	OS Pathfinder 678, 679 and 688; OS Landranger 102
Time allowed:	1: Shorter walk: Between 2 and 3 hours
	2: Via Moss Side: Between 2 and 3½ hours
Conditions and difficulties:	Walking boots should be sufficient except after prolonged rain or in winter when Wellington boots would be preferable
Facilities:	There is a substantial village shop close to the green, and a public house, the Grapes, opposite
Public transport:	There is a bus service from Preston and Blackpool

1 Shorter walk: For a walk of no more than 5 miles take the exit from the green diagonally opposite from the church, along the winding road that leads towards Lytham. At the edge of the village, and just beyond a right-hand bend, turn left along a farm track which eventually comes to an end at a gate on our left. Before reaching the gate we press ahead, along a grassy track to the side, until it peters out at a fence. Take a stile to the right of the fence and, once over this stile, keep to the left-hand boundary of the field and continue under the power cables to the far left corner. Take the stile located a few yards in from the corner to emerge, shortly, in the next field. Now proceed along the boundary to our right and continue to the far right-hand corner where a stile leads us onto a quiet lane. Turn left and follow the directions from 4 below.

2 Via Moss Side: Walk across the green to the pond in the corner and, with your back to the church, keep to the left of the pond and look out for the cul-de-sac opposite, known as Mill Lane. The name comes from the, now, sailless windmill that we soon encounter. Follow this lane past the tennis club and the windmill, now a private residence, on the left to reach a farm. Carry on, straight ahead through the farmyard, and out into attractive open countryside. It should be possible to see Blackpool Tower a little to the right and the keen eye may also pick out Marton windmill. Beyond the field to the right is the branch line to Lytham and Blackpool South. Since leaving the farm we have remained on an enclosed track but this peters out at a field.

At this point the signs indicate that we should proceed straight ahead along the right-hand edge and then round the field corner to a footbridge. This is the logical way forward but the legal right of way is, in fact, by turning left on entering the field, alongside the hedge, until having passed under the power lines, turn right to maintain the previous direction across the field. Aim initially for the

– 47 –

Fylde Coast and Country Walks

pylon beyond the far side of the field but then, as we get closer, adjust the direction slightly to aim a little to the right of it and the footbridge should be found. Cross over Wrea Brook and aim for the farm buildings, the tops of which should be visible ahead. From the brow of the field press ahead towards the farm and pass through two gates before continuing round to a level crossing. Cross the line and proceed through the farm but, when faced with a gate ahead, turn left and down the farm's access road. Eventually it bends sharp right but we continue straight ahead, over a stile to the right of a gateway, and along the left-hand edge of a field. Skirt round the pond ahead and then continue as before to vacate the field at a gate.

3 Turn left onto Lytham Road and re-cross the single track railway at Moss Side station. This is a fairly busy road but there is a pavement taking us past a caravan site and over Wrea Brook again before eventually arriving at a junction with Corka Lane, opposite a small housing development that occupies the site of a former hospital. Turn right along this quiet lane where care is required as there is no pavement. At the next T-junction turn left into Bryning Hall Lane. This road rises to a crest from where the windmill and church at Wrea Green can be seen on the left. Beyond the brow a quicker return to Wrea Green can be followed by looking out on the left for a stile to the left of a gate and then following the instructions in 5 below.

4 Continue round the right-hand corner to pass farms on either side of this quiet, winding road before reaching Bryning Lane, a busy road between Wrea Green and Warton. As there are bends both ways on this road care is needed when crossing straight over to pass the Equitation Centre on the right. Continue through

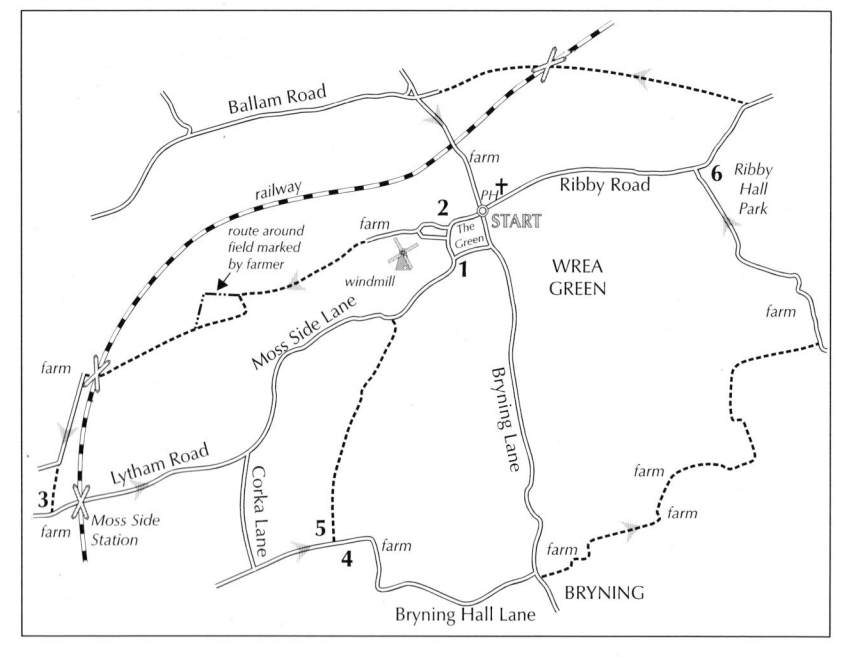

Walk 10: Around Wrea Green

The pond at Wrea Green

Hill Farm and, once again, into open countryside. We pass by two more small farms but, after passing the second of these, Prospect Farm on the left, continue along an enclosed track before it expires at fields ahead. Take the wicket gate on the left and continue ahead, by the right-hand edge of the field, to a corner and follow it round, passing a pond on the right, until the next corner where a stile will be seen a few yards to the left. On a clear day there are panoramic views eastwards to Winter Hill, Pendle Hill in the centre and the Lancashire fells. Continue along the right-hand edge of the next field, with the ditch on the right, to reach another stile in the corner. Negotiating this to pass into the next field we proceed for just a few yards before taking the footbridge and stile on our right.

Changing direction we are now facing roughly eastwards towards Pendle Hill in the distance. We need to keep along the right-hand edge to the end of the field where a stile is crossed by a gate. Continue ahead with the hedge now on our left until reaching a ladder stile by a gate. This brings us out onto a made-up farm road. Turn left to follow the road through a farm and, as it changes direction to the left, look back for extensive views to the south which, on a clear day, can encompass the Welsh hills. The road soon bends right and left at which point the chalet buildings of the Ribby Leisure Complex can be seen ahead. Before long the lane curves to the right and drops down, passing Ribby Hall Holiday Village on the right. Eventually we reach Ribby Road where we can either turn right and follow the directions from section 6 or turn left for the remaining half mile or so to Wrea Green.

5 Once over the stile proceed along the left-hand edge of the field towards Wrea Green. Continue to the far left-hand corner where a stile will be located leading

us into another field. Now follow the right-hand edge this time and continue, beyond the power lines, to the far right-hand corner of the field where, a few yards left of the corner, a stile leads on to an enclosed path. Within a few yards it joins a broader farm track which continues beyond a copse to eventually emerge onto a road. Turn right here to return the short distance back to the green.

6 After turning right from Brown's Lane it is a short distance, past the entrance to the Ribby Hall Holiday Village, to find a ladder stile on the other side of the road. From the stile we need to aim half-left along a faint path towards the small copse nearest to us in this large field. Keep to the right of the copse to reach a stile and then follow the right-hand boundary of the next field. From here pass through an open gateway to a stile. The hedge is now on our left as we continue in the same direction to a stile leading to an enclosed grassy track. At the far end ignore the stile on the left and proceed into the field ahead aiming a little to the left to locate a further stile, bringing us to the railway. Cross the branch line and turn left for a few yards to reach the stile on the far side.

The raised mound ahead of us is a covered reservoir but we must now strike half-left towards a group of buildings. As we draw nearer keep right of a clump of trees to reach a stile leading onto an access road. Now walk up to the junction at Fox Lane Ends, noting the wayside cross here. Turn left and follow the road over the railway bridge; Wrea Green station used to be sited to the right of the bridge. Soon we are back at the green with the Grapes on the left and the old village pump ahead.

WALK 11

Around Warton

An incongruous mix of estuary, farmland and, possibly, fighter planes encountered on this walk.

Distance:	4½ miles
Start:	From Bank Lane, off the south side of Lytham Road, about ⅓ mile west of Church Road traffic lights. Grid reference: 405282
Map:	OS Pathfinder 688 and 678; OS Landranger 102
Time allowed:	2 hours
Conditions and difficulties:	Walking boots should prove suitable for all weathers
Facilities:	While there are no facilities on the walk itself, there is a store and other shops in Warton, together with a pub
Public transport:	There is a regular bus service between Preston, Lytham and Blackpool

1 Start walking away from the main road down Bank Lane but note the short road on the left known as Ferrier Bank. It is named after the famous singer Kathleen Ferrier who lived nearby on Bank Lane for a while. Soon we leave the houses behind and emerge into rural surroundings of old farms and cottages. Over to the left is the airfield of British Aerospace, opened in 1942 as Warton Air Depot and becoming Base Air Depot 2 (or BAD 2) while under American control during 1943 to 1945. It is difficult to imagine now but, during the War there were ten thousand men working here around the clock on overhauls, modifications and general maintenance on aircraft and equipment and, in the process, giving vital support to the United States 8th and 9th Air Forces. On occasion there were as many as eight hundred planes on the airfield at one time. The road twists and

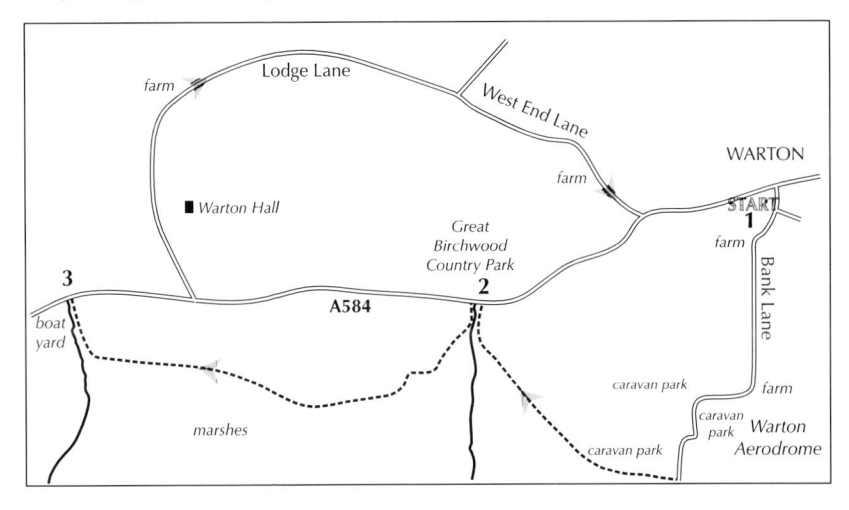

– 51 –

Fylde Coast and Country Walks

Bank Lane, Warton

turns, passing farms and caravan sites until straightening out beyond Seaview Caravan Site to face the Ribble estuary, with Southport visible ahead and also Winter Hill on a clear day.

On reaching a T-junction turn right along the Lancashire Coastal Way and pass Sea View Cottage and farm to arrive at a stile. Our way now is along a broad grassy track. To our left, sets of guiding lights stretch out across the creeks for the benefit of the many planes, including fighter planes, whose flight path into Warton aerodrome this is. Continue along the embankment past a line of hawthorn trees on the right to reach a kissing gate. Straight ahead, the embankment continues in the open between the creeks and fields while a little to the left in the distance Lytham windmill and the spire of St John the Divine can be seen. The line of debris deposited on our left gives some idea of how high the water reaches at the highest tides. On approaching a cottage and just as the grassy track curves to the left to some gates, follow a narrow track towards a stile in front of the cottage. Beyond the stile, turn right around the hedge on the right and follow the driveway, past the cottage, and onwards to the main road where a stile to the right of gates leads onto the pavement.

2 Turn left across the bridge over the brook and, immediately on the other side of the bridge, climb the concrete steps and then drop down to a narrow path running away from the road. The path (which can be overgrown in summer) continues alongside the brook until meeting a further short flight of concrete steps leading to a stile on the right. Beyond the stile, head along the embankment out towards the estuary. Before long the track swings round to resume its course alongside the creeks and towards Lytham. Over to the right are the fields of Lodge Farm

Walk 11: Around Warton

Boat yard at Lytham

opposite the next stile. Further on, another stile is reached just before crossing a farm track that drops down onto the creeks. Continue ahead through a gateway and along the embankment to approach Lytham's boat yards. The track swings to the right on reaching an inlet creek of a brook simply entitled Main Drain, lined up with boats adjoining jetties. Follow the track round to the right to reach Dock Bridge.

3 Once through the gate turn right onto the pavement alongside the main road. On reaching the first road on the left, Lodge Lane, cross over and proceed down the quiet lane through farmland. Soon we pass the imposing gates of Warton Hall on the right with its solid high red-brick wall. There are other more modest houses on the left, also with grounds to spare, and Warton Hall Farm entrance on the right. Across the fields to the left the level alignment of the railway to Blackpool can be seen. On passing Carr Farm on the left we resume our journey through open countryside; just isolated trees, small woods, hedges, fields (some undulating) and the occasional farm building. At the junction with Carr Lane on the left, just beyond the bridge over Wrea Brook, continue straight ahead along what is now West End Lane with the houses of Warton ahead and the BAe factory beyond. Follow the road (the old road to Lytham) round to the right and past Brook Farm before bending to the left, through a residential area, to reach the main road again. Behind the houses on the left side of West End Lane once stood the Base Air Depot's hospital. Turn left onto the main road and Bank Lane will soon be found on the right.

– 53 –

WALK 12

Freckleton

A walk around one of the older villages on the Fylde whose fortunes have been bound up to the Ribble estuary and, more recently, the nearby aerodrome. It was the scene of one of the greatest tragedies of the Second World War.

Distance:	4 miles
Start:	From the car park on Preston Old Road in the centre of the village. Grid reference: 432290
Map:	OS Pathfinder 688; OS Landranger 102
Time allowed:	2 hours
Conditions and difficulties:	It is preferable to wear Wellington boots because, even in dry conditions, the side of the estuary may be muddy, especially if there has been a recent high tide
Facilities:	Public houses and shops in the village
Public transport:	There is a regular bus service between Preston, Lytham St Annes and Blackpool

1 From the car park turn left onto Preston Old Road, past the library and the primary school on the left, and continue beyond the mini roundabout, with Naze Lane East on the right, until approaching a left-hand bend where Bunker Street

The Ship at Freckleton

− 54 −

Walk 12: Freckleton

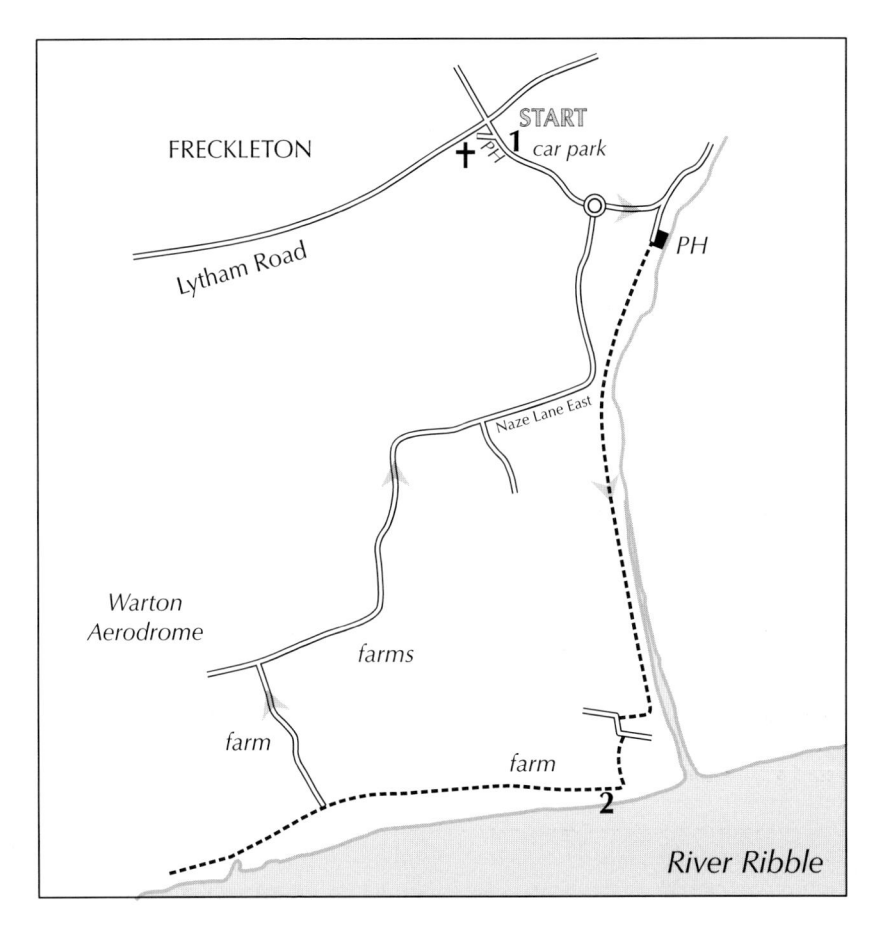

will be seen on the right. Turn into Bunker Street passing cottages associated with the boating industry that once thrived here. The name of the street refers to the coal bunkers nearby that were used to store coal delivered by boats from Wigan, along the river Douglas and across the Ribble to Freckleton. A little further on the left is the Ship Inn, known to date from at least the seventeenth century but thought to have a history as old as the fourteenth century. From the car park of the Ship, there is a fine panoramic view eastwards, on a clear day, to Longridge Fell, Pendle Hill in the distance, and Winter Hill, with its mast. The office blocks and football stadium at Preston can also be seen and, likewise, Jubilee Tower, overlooking Darwen. The Ship Inn is a reminder of Freckleton's importance as a port and, later, a shipbuilding centre until the nineteenth century.

The path becomes rougher beyond the inn and where it appears to veer off to the right, forge straight ahead across a drive, keeping to the left of a house, to emerge onto an enclosed path. Soon the creeks will be seen below, home to small boatyards. A road draws near on the right but ignore the stile at this point. Down below, to the left, one can see signs of a former embankment designed

Fylde Coast and Country Walks

to hold back flood waters. Shortly, the path meets an access road that drops down to the creeks. Walk briefly up this road and, where it swings round to the right into a yard, keep left through a kissing gate and proceed, across a private drive, along a narrow path. This path continues over a footbridge and past some houses before arriving at a private parking area with a steep descent to the left. Proceed ahead to a path running left of a large field. Go through the kissing gate to enjoy the extensive views that, once again, open up.

Where the path divides a few yards further on, ignore the one dropping down to the left but continue at the same level. When conditions permit the Lancashire fells can be seen from Parlick at the southern end towards Grizedale Fell and Clougha further north. A succession of footbridges is encountered while maintaining the same direction until approaching the white house known as Naze Cottage. On reaching the garden use the stile to turn right along a narrow, enclosed path until emerging at the driveway to the cottage. Now turn left, taking the stile to the right of the cattle grid, at the entrance to the drive, to follow the narrow path that eventually emerges, via a stile, into a field. Keep to the right-hand edge of the field with the Ribble estuary ahead. At the far side there is a permissive path to a seat and triangulation point on the left from where there are excellent views. It is also a good spot to to watch the bird life. Directly across the river is the mouth of the river Douglas.

2 Returning to the path we must now pass through a kissing gate and drop down onto the creeks and turn right. When Preston Docks was open it was possible to see ocean-going vessels making their way along the Ribble on the tide but this came to an end when the docks closed in the early 1980s. Cross a stile below Naze Mount and pass the private access track that heads back up the embankment. This section can be very muddy so care is needed in choosing a suitable course along the side of the estuary. Now look out for a small headland as we shall need to leave the banks of the Ribble at that point. On reaching this small promontory a track will be seen in the hedge on the right. Cross a stile to gain access to this track, which is Pool Lane.

On passing beyond the boundary of a private house (to the left of the stile we have just crossed) the huge testing plants at British Aerospace, Warton, will be seen to the left. At a T-junction turn right, still on Pool Lane, through a small farming community tucked away at the back of the large aerodrome. A short distance beyond a left-hand corner the road becomes Bush Lane and then, later, Stoney Lane. Good views can be obtained of what was once the longest runway in Europe. Whereas now the aerodrome is used for manufacturing components for defence aircraft such as the Tornado, during World War Two it was an American Airforce Base known as Base Air Depot 2 (Burtonwood being known as BAD 1) specializing in work on the P–51 Mustangs and B–24 Liberators amongst many other types of aircraft. Eventually there follows a straight stretch leading to a left-hand bend where the outward path can be seen through the hedge.

Beyond the bend we continue into a built-up area on the outskirts of Freckleton along Naze Lane East to a mini roundabout. Note the last house on the right with its cobbled yard and small barn to the rear. It has a datestone of 1780. Turn left here to return along what was once the main road to Preston from Lytham.

Walk 12: Freckleton

There is a variety of housing stock along this road including the diminutive cottages on the left and look out for the sundial set into the gable wall of an end-of-terrace opposite Richardson Close. Before returning to the car park walk on to the centre of the village, past the small building on the right with a conical roof that is the former District Bank premises built in 1913. It stands on the site of the old smithy. Behind is the old green that is now the Memorial Garden to the War Dead, a reminder that one of the most tragic accidents of the last war occurred in the village when an American Liberator bomber took off from Warton airfield in a thunderstorm and crashed into the village school killing a total of 61 people including 38 children and 2 teachers in August 1944. The former school was situated on land now occupied by the houses of Trinity Close between the Coach and Horses and the church. A monument to the victims, that is worth seeing, stands at the rear of Holy Trinity church, just round the corner. Now retrace one's steps to the car park.

WALK 13

From Kirkham

Through open countryside north of Kirkham and return along an ancient track. The town trail offers plenty of interest.

Distance:	6¼ miles
Start:	From Kirkham station. Grid reference: 419326
Map:	OS Pathfinder 679; OS Landranger 102
Time allowed:	3 hours
Conditions and difficulties:	Walking boots should be sufficient for the longer walk but note that in field corners especially it can be very muddy
Facilities:	Various in Kirkham centre
Public transport:	Apart from the trains there is a regular bus service from Preston, Blackpool and Fleetwood

1 From the station, heading away from the town centre (or if travelling by train turning right outside the station), take the second turning on the right named Derby Road. The road name is not very clear but note Wesham Park Hospital here which we pass on our left as we make our way down to the far end of the road at Butterworth Close, a cul-de-sac. Take the footpath alongside the close to reach a stile ahead leading into a field. Continue in a straight line to pass a pond on the right. From here there are clear views of the railway and the parish church with its fine crocketed spire. On reaching the field boundary turn left to go over a stile and along an enclosed section of the field. Having reached a brow drop down towards a stile and continue, in the same direction, towards a wood until reaching a stile in the fence on the right. Cross over and then immediately resume the previous direction, keeping the fence on our left. Maintain a straight course to the right of the wood to arrive, via a stile, at a road. Now turn right to pass the entrance to a caravan park. A few yards further on a public footpath sign and a stile on the left invite us to enter a wood.

Cut straight through the woods to a track on the other side where a stile leads into a field. Veer slightly left across the field to reach a stile over a fence into the next field and here cross half-right. On reaching the crest of the field a new vista opens up. In the distance the fells can be seen while the masts of the Ministry of Defence communications station and the M55 motorway are in the foreground. Just ahead, and surrounded by bushes, is a pool in the middle of the field. Keep to the right of it before dropping down to a stile in the fence ahead and left of the Communication Station masts ahead. Crossing over into a field corner walk along the left-hand edge and at another fence corner, a few yards away, continue ahead to the brow of the field with the M55 now clearly visible. Veer slightly to the right to locate a ladder stile in a fence and then turn right alongside a hedge to a footbridge. Now follow the left-hand boundary of the field to reach a stile by a gate in the far left corner. Follow the right-hand edge of the next field to a stile leading to the steps of the motorway bridge. Take great

Walk 13: From Kirkham

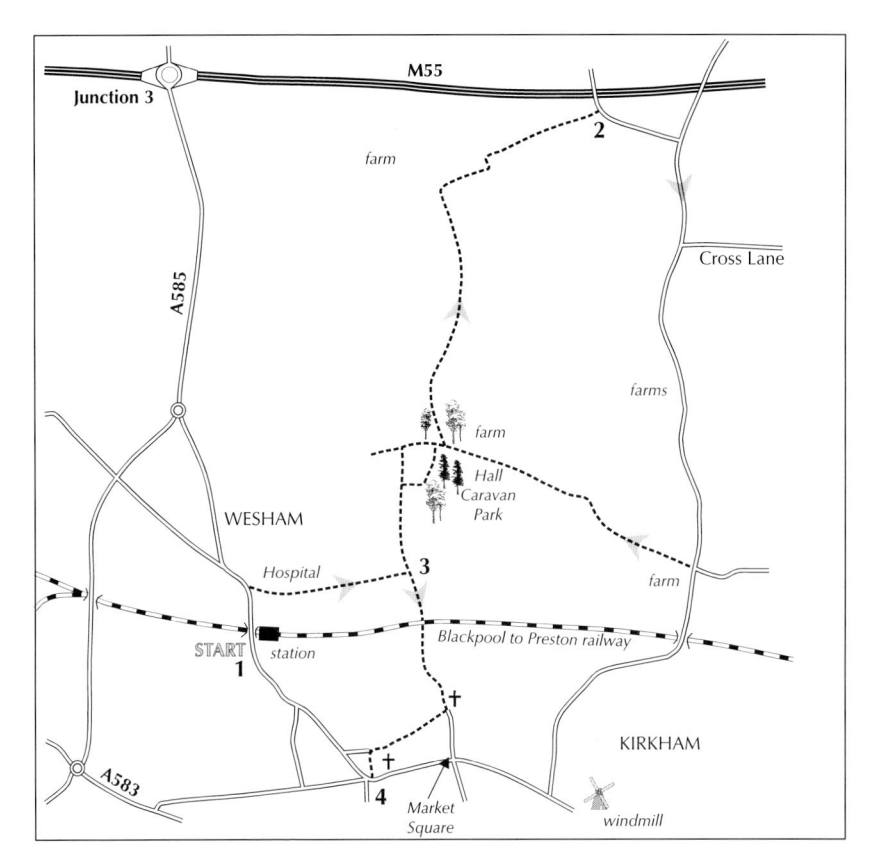

care in reaching the steps as, during the growing season, the brambles and nettles can be formidable.

2 Turn right along the farm road which leads to a country lane at a T-junction. We now maintain a reasonably straight course for the next mile down this lane, known as Moorside, in the heart of pleasant unspoilt countryside. As there is no pavement care is required at all times especially if there are children. Although this is a farming area it is noticeable that some of the farms that we pass have been converted to residential use. At the junction with Cross Lane look out for the picturesque, single-storey, thatched cottage on the corner. It is one of a number in the area. Continue to the next junction with the Kirkham road where a sharp right turn is made, initially towards a farm, but remaining to its right along the bridleway. This is an ancient track and also attractive, especially in spring or early summer when birds and butterflies are busy in the high hedges and there is a variety of wild flowers on either side. Before the track drops down look through the gaps in the hedges on the left for a good view of Kirkham. The windmill (now in residential use) is on the left, St Michael's Church in the centre of the view and Wesham to the far right, where much of the town's industrial base is situated. Eventually, Mowbreck Hall Farm is reached on the right with

Fylde Coast and Country Walks

Cottage at Cross Lane near Kirkham

Mowbreck Manor on the left. The manor stands on the site of the old hall, once the home of the Westby family for over three hundred years and later acquired by the Earl of Derby. Just beyond the caravan site entrance take the stile left of a gate and proceed along a narrow path. At a footbridge across a brook turn right and skirt around the small copse until it curves round, parallel to the fence ahead. At this point head straight across to the fence and over a stile. Now turn left towards the brow and re-enter an enclosed section via a stile. At the top of the incline Kirkham's skyline appears ahead.

3 Drop down to a stile and aim for the tunnel under the railway. Another stile will be encountered at the bottom of the field in the left-hand corner and having crossed this go forward to a stile by the tunnel. The track passes under the railway and leads directly to the Church of St Michael which, though dating from 1822, occupies the site of previous churches. Indeed, the parish registers date back to 1539 and within the church there is a medieval font. Outwardly, the most striking aspect of the church is its tower with recessed spire, decorated with crockets and supported by flying buttresses. It has been described as one of the finest in Lancashire. At the church we need to turn right to enter a park next to the cemetery. On the left is the Memorial Garden, dedicated to the town's war dead. Continue onto Barnfield and note the road on the right, Flaxfield, a reminder of the flax mill that was established here in 1732, becoming Birley and Sons who employed 1600 workers. The mill was demolished in 1972 and the land now occupied by the supermarket. Turn left through the supermaket car park and onto Mill Street for the town trail unless a quicker return is required in which case

Walk 13: From Kirkham

continue along Barnfield to the T-junction and turn right towards the station, less than half a mile away.

4 From Mill Street turn left into Poulton Street but note on the corner the lamp that has been refurbished by Kirkham and Rural Fylde Rotary Club. It was originally erected by the inhabitants of Kirkham in 1887 to commemorate Queen Victoria's Golden Jubilee. It is worth noting, as we walk up the hill, that some of the offices are conversions of former houses of substance but, as will be seen further on in Preston Street, there is quite a variety of housing stock, from the town houses of the industrialists to weavers' cottages. Having reached the brow of the hill we now descend to the Market Square where the 'fishstones' have been retained. These are flat stone slabs supported on stone from where fish was once sold on market days. Note the old lamp here with a plaque to mark the 700th anniversary of the granting of the Charter in 1296 when Kirkham became a Free Borough and was able to run markets and fairs. Another substantial house stands across Church Street from the Square. Ash Tree House is a three-storey, five-bay property that was built in the eighteenth century for the Langton family, prominent industrialists in Kirkham.

Continue up Preston Street and note the Stables on the right and the Black Horse on the left. The latter was a coaching inn with the stabling area at the back, through the arch. There is a pleasing mixture of smaller dwellings and grander houses such as the one occupied by Hillside Restaurant, with steps on either side leading to a grand doorway and pillars with a lamp above the steps. At the top of the hill note the former windmill at about the highest point in Kirkham, close to where a former Roman encampment was situated. Now return along the other side of the road for a closer view of Hillside, built in 1801 for William Birley, owner of the flax mill, and owned by the family until 1934. Look out too for the former weavers' cottages with stone steps and bricked-up cellar windows near which handlooms were once placed. There is also a limited amount of sympathetic infilling of new buildings which helps to retain, as much as possible, the character of this thoroughfare. At Market Square either continue into Poulton Street or return via Church Street where there are some old cottages which would, almost certainly, have been thatched at one time. Turn left by the church and pass the Memorial Gardens, once again, and continue along Barnfield to the T-junction. Turn right here for the station.

WALK 14

Salwick and Treales

A pleasant walk that offers quiet lanes and towpaths while keeping in touch with anthems of the modern world such as the motorway and nuclear power.

Distance:	4 or 6 miles
Start:	From the lay-by immediately south of Salwick station. Grid reference: 463319
Maps:	OS Pathfinder 679; OS Landranger 102
Time allowed:	Three hours (Shorter walk 2¼ hours)
Conditions and difficulties:	Walking boots should be sufficient except after periods of prolonged rain when Wellington boots would be preferable. One or two stiles may cause difficulty in summer due to encroaching brambles and nettles
Facilities:	The Hand and Dagger is clearly visible above the canal north of Salwick while the Derby Arms can be found in the centre of Treales
Public transport:	There is a sparse train service at the time of writing and there is a bus service from Blackpool and Preston

1 From the lay-by cross over the railway bridge and continue along the footpath, noting one of the dwindling number of traditional signal boxes on the right. Continue round the first right-hand bend but, if the shorter walk is preferred, take the stile on the left and follow the instructions under 6 below. Otherwise, continue less than 100 yards beyond the next left-hand bend and cross over in order to enter the yard beside the Lancaster Canal where there are mooring points for boats.

2 We now turn left onto the canal towpath. Follow a tree-lined course to the next road bridge by the side of which stands the Hand and Dagger Inn. The inn takes its name from the emblem on the Clifton family coat of arms, the Cliftons being substantial landowners in the area at one time. Built at the same time as the canal it has served the users of the waterway ever since and, in times past, its stables were used for changing horses that used the towpath. This was especially necessary for the fast 'fly boats', long narrow boats that operated the service between Preston and Kendal when horses needed to be changed every few miles.

Beyond the bridge the towpath walk continues under the shade of the trees, the source of much birdsong, particularly in spring. On approaching the next bridge look out for the milestone recording that Garstang is 11 miles away and Preston 6 miles. This explains the name of bridge 27, also known as Six Mile Bridge. Now the trees give way to hedgerows and open countryside while the background hum of the motorway traffic becomes more audible. Beyond bridge 28, that carries another farm track, the M55 motorway can be seen for the first

– 62 –

Walk 14: Salwick and Treales

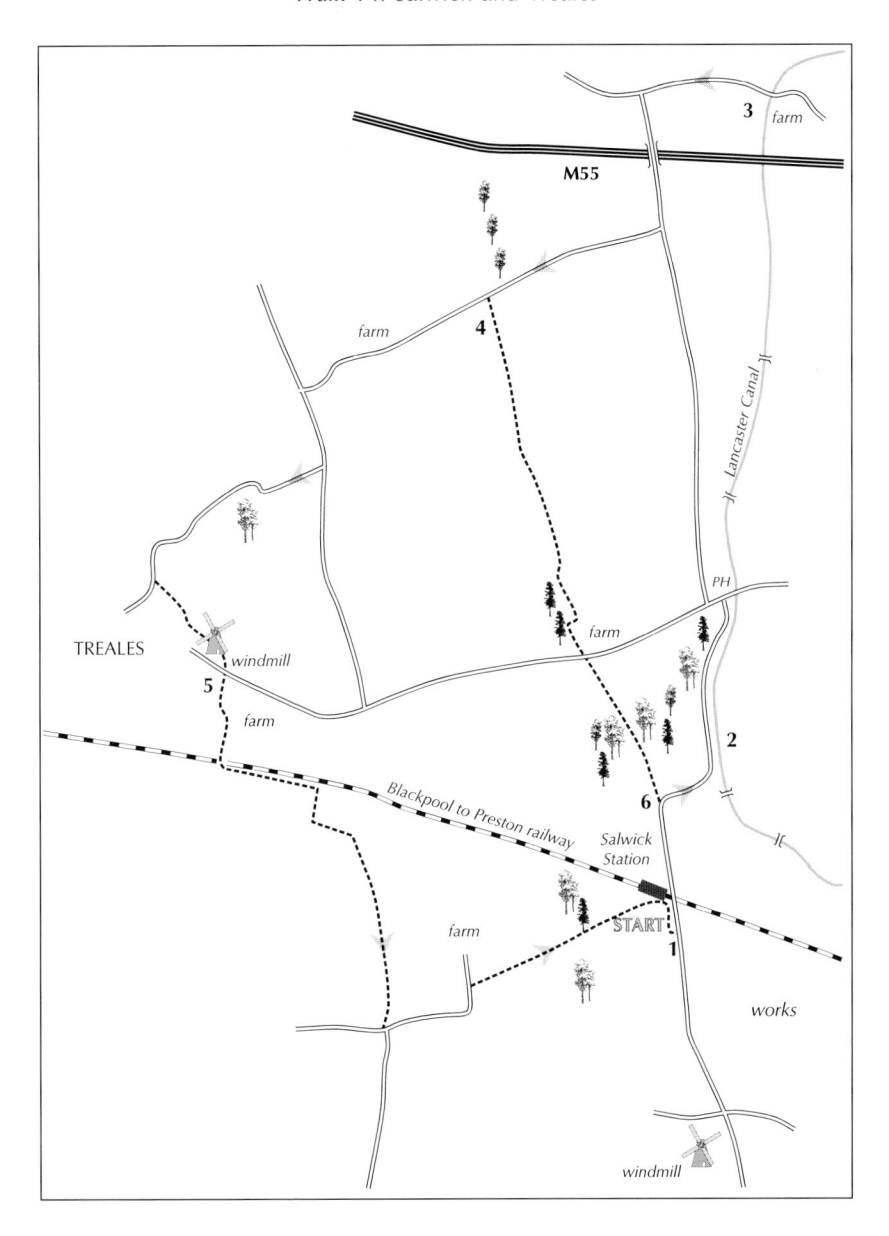

time. The motorway bridge provides a massive contrast with the pleasing curves of the standard canal bridges and, having passed under it, the end of the canal section is in sight at Kellet's Bridge.

3 Leave the canal at bridge 29 and, emerging onto a quiet lane, turn left. The masts of the radio transmission station at Inskip are now clearly visible across the fields to our right and the keen eye may also pick out Inskip church spire in the same

Kellet's Bridge

general direction. Soon we take the first left turn beyond the house on the right-hand side and cross over the motorway this time. Looking left from the bridge one can see Longridge Fell and, behind it, Pendle Hill.

With the motorway behind us we take the first turning right into Moss Lane East and continue to the wood on the right beyond Stanley Grange. At a point level with the far end of the wood look out for a public footpath sign and a stile in the hawthorn hedge on the left-hand side of the road as this affords a quick and relatively straight route back to Salwick.

4 Continue up the road, passing Moss House Farm to reach a junction. Kirkham lies directly ahead but out of sight in a dip, a reminder of how undulating this area is rather than the flat landscape it is often perceived to be. We now need to turn left along a lane that is enclosed by hedges but before long we arrive at the next junction and turn right into Moss Lane West, another reminder of the former landscape in these parts before widespread draining of the mosses was undertaken. As we walk along this quiet lane note the sail-less windmill at Treales on the left (though it will be more difficult to see in summer due to tree foliage). We pass a pond on the right and then a wood on our left and, on approaching power cables, look out for a public footpath sign on the right. Do not follow it but, just a little further, is a second sign on the left at a right-hand bend.

Passing through the gate, proceed ahead and keep by the hedge on the right. For those with good eyesight the church spire in the distance on the left is at Inskip. A second gate is negotiated from where we pass through a larger field. Following the hedge round to the right we come face to face with the windmill at Treales. Eventually, a stile is reached in the far right-hand corner and a second

Walk 14: Salwick and Treales

stile a little further on. The windmill is now immediately on our right towering above us. Thought to date from about 1830 it is a four-storey mill which, since the 1960s, has been a private residence. From the stile go half-right to a stone stile, by the side of the windmill, to emerge onto a courtyard serving the former mill and associated cottages. Follow the drive away to its junction with the road leading to the centre of the village, believed to be one of the oldest on the Fylde. It is a short diversion along the road to the right to the Derby Arms, a reminder of the formidable presence of the Earls of Derby who owned large tracts of land in this area. The earldom was given to Lord Stanley by Henry Tudor following the Battle of Bosworth in 1485 and, soon after, the Stanley family acquired large confiscated estates both north and south of the Ribble. The family name of Stanley is also frequently encountered on the Fylde for this reason.

5 Assuming a refreshment break is not required, cross the road and take the gate ahead into a field. Veer half-left to locate another stile in a section of the field that protrudes away from the general boundary line. Once over this stile continue in the same direction up the next field to reach another stile and a gate leading onto the footbridge over the Preston-Blackpool main railway line. There is quite an extensive view from this point from where it is possible to see three windmills. To the left of the bridge the mill at Clifton, tallest on the Fylde, can be seen (follow the line of pylons). To the right Kirkham windmill is visible, surrounded by houses, while behind us, of course, is the mill at Treales. Looking south along the railway note milepost 6, denoting the distance from Preston and, just visible with the naked eye beyond the next bridge south, is the station platform at Salwick.

Now cross the bridge and turn left keeping along the left-hand boundary and passing milepost 6, seen earlier from the bridge. Keep a watchful eye across to the far side of the field on the right for a footbridge and, on our left, for a public footpath badge on a post indicating a change of direction to our right. If neither the footbridge nor the badge are noticed bear in mind that we need to cross the field before the first pylon. Once across the bridge turn left to a field corner. Now cross another footbridge and stile to continue parallel to the railway as far as the next field corner. Here we must turn right with the ditch and head away from the railway. The field rises quite steeply before levelling off. Eventually a footbridge is crossed as we continue in the same direction to a left-hand field corner and round to a gate leading onto a quiet lane.

Turn left and then left again along a farm track leading to Dingle Farm. Continue round a sharp left-hand corner and, before reaching the next bend, take a gate on the right in the hedge and aim for the right-hand edge of the woods ahead, beyond the power cables. On drawing level with the wood on the left cross a stile by a gate. Salwick station can be seen ahead and we should now strike out across the field towards the far end of the station and to the left of the houses ahead. In the far left-hand corner of the field, almost beside the station platform, a stile will be found where there was once a kissing gate. Go forward to a second stile and then follow the track on the right back to the lay-by. Beyond the lay-by stands the large British Nuclear Fuels complex that has dominated this village since 1945.

6 Take the stile on the left and continue in the same direction through the field towards the woods. Having mounted the brow of the field it is not easy to see

the stile at the edge of the woods at first but, as long as the same direction is maintained, the stile should be located. The passage through the woods is brief with a footbridge crossing before emerging, via a stile, into a field. Keep straight ahead along the right-hand edge to reach a road. Cross over to a stile leading us into a field beside a farm. Continue in the same direction as before towards a wood and, on reaching it, walk round to the right of it and then maintain the previous direction keeping the wood on our left. On reaching the field boundary follow it round to a gate and then, in the next field, maintain the prevailing direction towards the aerials of the wireless station at Inskip. We now pass two ponds fringed with trees on the left and a further pond on the right but keep closer to those on the left as it will help to keep us on track for the stile (it looks like part of the fence at first glance) in the far boundary. Once into the next field we can see the traffic on the M55 ahead but our north-westerly progress will come to a halt before reaching the motorway. Continuing along the right-hand edge of a large field look ahead to another wood. We shall be changing direction on reaching it but, for now, it is necessary to negotiate another stile at a boundary leading us into the next field and then, half way along its right-hand boundary, we are joined by a ditch on our right. At the far right-hand corner a stile takes us onto a quiet road, a short distance from Stanley Grange on the right. Now turn left and follow the directions under section 4.

WALK 15

South of Preston

A fascinating excursion exploring some historic parts of the area south of the city centre. There is a surprisingly rural feel to sections of this walk.

Distance:	7½ miles
Start:	On Broadgate, immediately south of the junction with Strand Road and Fishergate Hill, to the west of the city centre. Spaces should be found without too much difficulty. Grid reference: 528285
Map:	OS Pathfinder 688; OS Landranger 102; A-Z map of Preston
Time allowed:	3½ hours
Conditions and difficulties:	When dry, normal shoes may suffice but walking boots are always advisable as a minimum when passing through farmland as is the case on this walk. When wet, Wellington boots would be a better bet
Facilities:	All the usual facilities associated with a large town or city
Public transport:	There is a regular bus service operating along Fishergate Hill at the junction with Broadgate or, alternatively, one can walk from the railway station

1 Walk away from the traffic lights along the broad tree-lined road, aptly named Broadgate, to the first junction on the right. Bollards limit vehicular access over Old Penwortham Bridge, once the main road crossing over the Ribble on the west side of Preston but now enjoying a long quiet retirement. Our journey takes us over this historic bridge and, once on the other side, turn left alongside the river. Note the pipeline that crosses the river on the supports that once carried the former railway line to Southport. Further on, the girders of another bridge, carrying the West Coast Main Line, can be seen. At the end of the road, as we continue along a path next to the river, the slim spire of St Walburge can be seen over to the left. As we pass under the main railway line it can be seen that the viaduct has been widened beyond the original arches. The next bridge we pass under once carried the old Lancashire & Yorkshire route to Liverpool until it closed in 1972. Just beyond the bridge, turn right through a gate and follow the path up onto the embankment carrying the former line over the Ribble.

2 Turn right again and cross the bridge. At first it seems as if the way will be blocked by railings but, on reaching the apparent barrier, a way across will be seen to the right of the trackbed. From here there is an excellent view across to the main line on the left and the former tramroad on the right which we shall cross later. Once over the bridge drop down the steps, taking the first turning left just a little way down. This path enters Avenham Park. At the first junction turn left but notice the wide expanse of parkland ahead, complete with bandstand

Fylde Coast and Country Walks

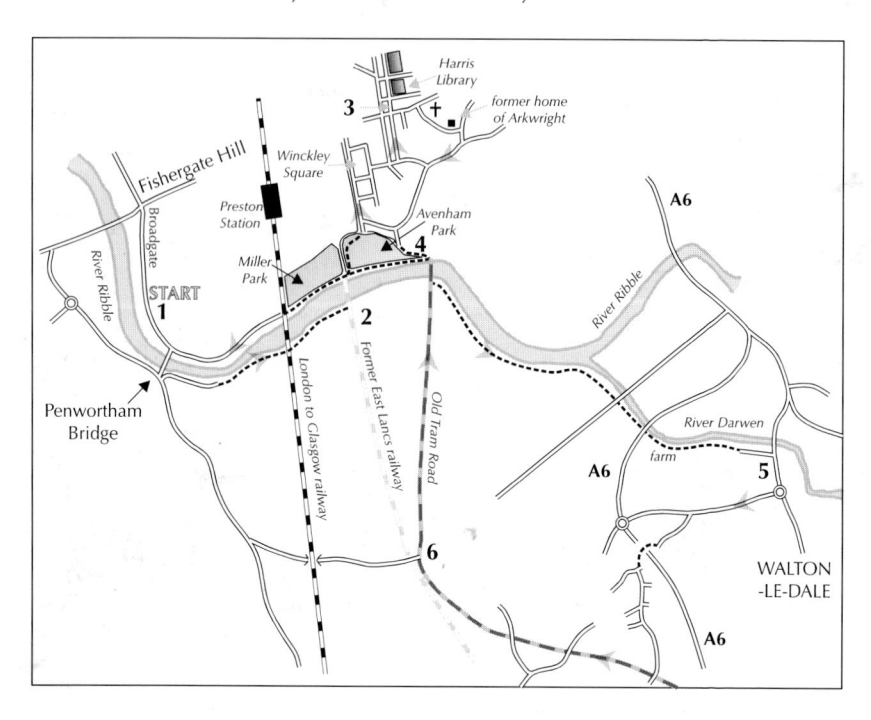

and events arena. It was here where the Spice Girls had their first public concert. Our path rises gently, passing a Japanese Rock Garden, complete with ornate wooden bridge on the right, before reaching a junction. To our left is a balustraded bridge that once carried the former East Lancashire Railway (ELR) to and from the city. We now need to turn right passing, on the left, a war memorial of pink granite to soldiers of the Loyal North Lancashire Regiment who lost their lives in the Boer War 1899-1902. Where the path splits take the left fork leading up to Ribblesdale Place, at which point we continue ahead.

Note the impressive houses of former generations of local gentry. Some have pillars and porticos while others have pilasters. On reaching Winckley Square turn right and then take the first gate on the left to enter the park. Proceed half-right along this splendid undulating park that contributes greatly to the overall visual attraction of the square, surely one of the finest outside London. We make our exit by the side of the imposing statue of Sir Robert Peel and continue along Cross Street, opposite the statue, to the far end with the multi-storey car park prominent ahead. Ignore the next left turn but take the second left instead, along Main Sprit Weind. A weind is an alleyway of which there are other examples in Garstang and the narrow width of this street would have been in keeping with the typical widths of medieval times. Now it is just an overlooked back street that leads us to the junction of Fishergate and Church Street.

Cross straight over into Birley Street and the massive portico of Harris Library will be seen ahead. Once at the edge of the library we have arrived at Market Place. This is an historic part of Preston where James 1 was received in 1617 and, during the first Jacobite Rebellion of 1715, where James Edward Stuart was

Walk 15: South of Preston

Old Penwortham Bridge

proclaimed James III before the Jacobites were forced to surrender to Hanoverian troops. More recently, Queen Elizabeth II was welcomed here in 2002 to confer City Status on Preston. The obelisk on the left was erected in 1979 to commemorate 800 years of Preston's history while, ahead, stands the War Memorial designed by Sir Giles Gilbert Scott.

3 Return along Birley Street, past Miller Arcade on the left and, at Church Street, turn left and note the narrow streets and courtyards on the other side – Old Cock Yard, Bolton's Court and the yard of the Old Bull – reminders of Preston's long history and, perhaps, holding the potential for future retail use in the same way that the Shambles does in York. The Old Bull Inn is at least of seventeenth-century vintage and its customers included Judge Jefferies, Bonnie Prince Charlie and Charles Dickens. During the 1820 election it was also the scene of violence when the mayor tried to read the Riot Act to supporters of Henry Hunt and had to be rescued by a troop of dragoons. On arriving at the largely nineteenth-century parish church, St John the Divine, take the right turn before the church into Stoneygate, one of Preston's five original medieval gates. The present church was built in 1853 but it stands on an ancient site. Stoneygate is pedestrianised to begin with but, as it develops into a road, look back for a better perspective of the church. At the bottom end of Stoneygate, once the main road south to the Ribble, look out on the left for the three-storey house that once was occupied by Sir Richard Arkwright while in the process of developing his famous water frame.

At the junction with Shepherd Street turn right into Syke Hill and then right again into Avenham Lane. Continue as far as the Avenham Harris Institute on the right, an impressive classical building of 1849 with a sweeping balustraded staircase, originally built as the Institution for the Diffusion of Knowledge to help educate working people. We must now turn left, opposite this building, along a broad tree-lined gravelly avenue known as Avenham Walks, originally laid out in the seventeenth century. This elegant road had, by 1728, become a fashionable promenade. Bushell Place, the road on the left, was named after Doctor William Bushell, former owner of the land, and who lived at Goosnargh, but perhaps the most eye-catching properties are the stuccoed Italianate villas of Tower House, Avenham Tower and Avenham Lodge, built in 1847. Avenham Tower was the home of Edwin Henry Booth, founder of Booths the grocers. From Avenham Lodge look left along Bank Parade, another impressive street of nineteenth-century houses. Joseph Livesey, founder of the Temperance Society, lived at no.13 until his death in 1884.

4 Now proceed down the grand flights of steps and try and imagine the extensive views that could once be obtained from here, described by the Young Pretender, Charles Edward Stuart, as 'an enchanting spot'. Ahead of us stands a concrete bridge over the Ribble. It is a copy of the timber bridge of 1802 that carried a tramway, connecting the Leeds and Liverpool Canal at Walton Summit with the wharves of the Lancaster Canal in Preston, near Fishergate. The tramway was built to avoid the much greater expense of an aqueduct across the Ribble Valley. At the bottom of the steps turn right down the path towards the bridge. Before crossing it, however, look back and up into the park for a view of the Belvedere, built in 1865 of Italian design. It occupies the site of a stationary steam engine which pulled the wagons of coal along the tramway up the steep slope with a rope.

Cross the bridge and, at the far side, turn right down the steps leading to a path. Turn right again under the bridge to continue along a surfaced path. It is hard to believe that we are so close to a major urban centre at this point as fields give a semi-rural feel to this section of the walk. The suburb of Frenchwood can soon be seen on the left, across the river, as the path joins a farm track from the adjoining fields. However, the going remains firm as we round the bend to the sound of traffic on the A6 ahead. Just a little further on is the confluence of the river Ribble and river Darwen and upstream is Walton Bridge, once a major bridging point. Around an earlier bridge, situated 75 yards nearer, a decisive Civil War battle was fought in which the Parliamentarians led by Oliver Cromwell inflicted considerable loss of life on the retreating Royalists in the area known as Walton Flats. The path now turns away from the Ribble and, at a crossing of paths, continues ahead towards Walton Green. Just before a bridge carrying a by-pass over us take a pedestrian gate on the right leading us along a path under the bridge. At a gate at the far end proceed through the farmyard of Walton Hall Farm, still keeping the river Darwen on our left. Pass through the farmyard of the old red brick farmhouse and leave the rural aspects of the walk behind as the track soon becomes a road encountering a primary school and a delightful grouping of cottages at Walton Green including one on the left dated 1675.

5 At the far end we need to turn right along what used to be the main road south of Preston. Before doing so, however, go left and cross the bridge over the river

Walk 15: South of Preston

The Earl of Derby monument in Miller Park, Preston

Fylde Coast and Country Walks

Darwen. A little further on the left, and now used as a restaurant, is the former Unicorn Inn. It was from here that Cromwell planned his tactics that resulted in the decisive victory over Royalist troops nearby in 1648. Now return over the bridge but it is worth contemplating that along this route would have passed English and Scottish armies as well as the opposing forces during the Civil War. In later years it was an important coaching route and continued in this role with the arrival of the internal combustion engine. Since the completion of the motorway and, more recently, the bypass nearby this road has declined in importance. Proceed up to the roundabout and turn right into Hennel Lane.

At a junction, by woodland on the far side, turn left up a steep road and, as we approach the far end of what is, in fact, a cul-de-sac, note a paved path and cycle track climbing away to the right. Take this and cross over the by-pass. The path winds down to another cul-de-sac. Turn right here to a junction with Todd Lane North where we turn left and, at crossroads, go over, still on Todd Lane North. Continue until the road begins to dip down, just beyond Lime Kiln Cottage on the left. A cycling path off to the right marks the course of the former tramroad. If you look back across the road you can see the old embankment in the field. Proceed along the made-up path on the right which has a modern feel to it except for the old established hedges on either side. The straight sections may suggest to a historian that here was once a railway but, in all honesty, it looks more like a 'New Towns' walkway. The path crosses over estate roads and begins to curve to the right. All is modern housing along this length of the tramroad and only when the gradient begins to steepen on the edge of the Ribble valley does the picture change. With the houses behind us a former railway embankment joins us on the left. Just beyond there is a choice of three ways. In the centre is the Preston Junction Local Nature Reserve which climbs up onto the embankment of the former ELR and over to the left a path passes below what would have been a bridge on the line. Our route, however, is to the right, along the now tree-lined former tramroad.

6 As we proceed down the tramroad it is easier to feel that we are following the course of an old railway as the embankment pursues a course through the trees. Eventually we cross the Old Tram Bridge again and, at the far side, turn left (unless a closer view of the Belvedere is required) along a delightful tree-lined riverside path at the bottom of Avenham Park which sweeps up to the housing on the cliff. Passing under the ELR bridge we take the first path on our right to enter Miller Park and, shortly, the Earl of Derby monument at the top of a splendid double-sweeping staircase comes into view. It was unveiled in 1873 in the presence of a crowd of 40,000 people! In front of the monument is a fountain with four sculptured figures representing earth, air, fire and water. Leaving the park pass to the right of the white pergola seen on the way in. It was originally a feature of the Glasgow Garden Festival of 1988. The path soon rejoins the riverside path to pass under the railway bridge carrying the West Coast Main Line. Note the huge sandstone blocks in the supports. Beyond the bridge follow the river until Penwortham Bridge comes into view as we return to the start.

WALK 16

From Woodplumpton

A walk through typical Fylde farmland with a return along the Lancaster Canal

Distance:	2¾ miles
Start:	From the centre of Woodplumpton village. Grid reference: 501347
Maps:	OS Pathfinder 679; OS Landranger 102
Time allowed:	1½ hours
Conditions and difficulties:	Walking boots should be sufficient in drier conditions but otherwise Wellington boots would be preferable.
Facilities:	The Wheatsheaf public house and the village store in Woodplumpton
Public transport:	There is a regular bus service from Preston and Poulton

1 Head south, past the Post Office and village store on the left, as far as the church. On the way pass an old Fylde cottage with corrugated tin roof, St Anne's Church of England Primary School on the right, the Great War Memorial and the Wheatsheaf on the left, and Church House Farm with its porch bearing a modern datestone of 1702. This is brick with a black-and-white-style first storey. The

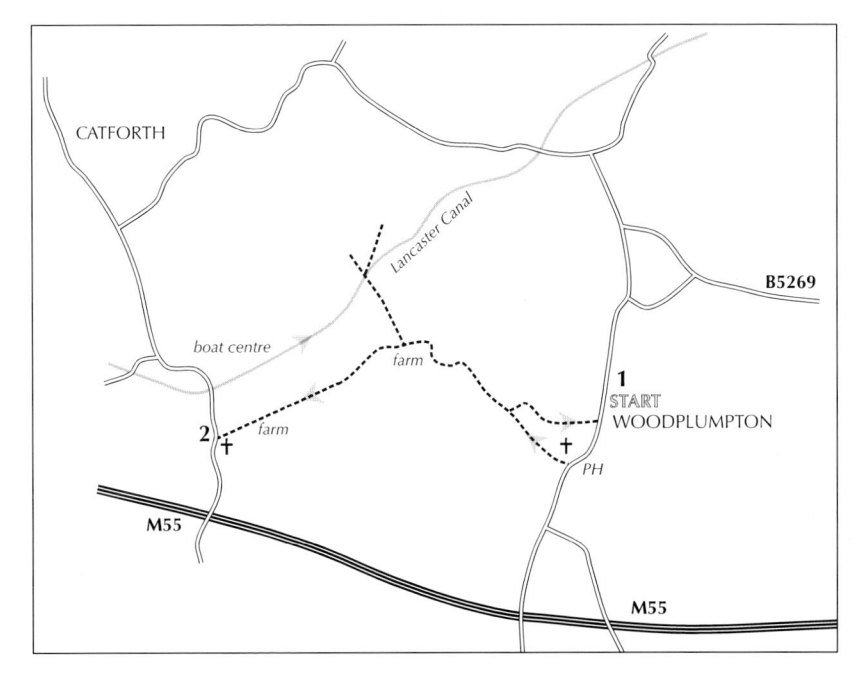

– 73 –

Cuckstool Farm at Woodplumpton

low-lying church of St Anne, crenellated above the wall, has stocks outside and a mounting block. Remnants of this church date as far back as the early fourteenth century but much of what is seen now is a product of both the sixteenth and eighteenth centuries. The weather vane atop the church has a fish as its motif. Pass through the lychgate and walk past the church noting on the left, just beyond the far end of the church, a boulder marking the traditional burial place of Meg Shelton, a reputed witch of the seventeenth century. Now look for a side path on the right that leads us, through a narrow gap, outside the churchyard. From here walk to the facing hedge and turn left to follow it round the bend, over a stile, and continue, ignoring gaps on the right, until reaching a gate leading onto a lane.

Having passed through the gate turn left along the quiet lane and follow it until it enters the yard of Whinnyfield Farm. Proceed to the far side and turn left through gates to follow the track away. Continue past farm buildings on the left and straight on, along what is initially a broad enclosed track, before opening out towards Woodplumpton Brook. A narrow footbridge should be located on the right-hand side. Cross this but, on advancing a few paces, keep to the left of a hedge in front and resume our previous direction with the hedge on our right. Where the field narrows at the far end to a gate, pass through and keep to the right of the next field until a further gate is negotiated. Proceed along a farm track and then a made-up road that passes farm buildings, including Crown Lane Farm, to eventually reach the main road with Crown Lane Free Methodist Church on the left at the junction.

2 Turn right and proceed along the lane but care is required as there is no footpath. However, it is a short distance to the bridge over the canal, just beyond Swillbrook House. Turn right beyond the bridge and into the boat centre and yard to follow

Walk 16: From Woodplumpton

the towpath, passing over Woodplumpton Brook on a modest aqueduct, until reaching the next bridge, number 34, over the canal. Take the stile on the left, before the bridge, and climb the steps to a farm track. Cross over the canal to follow the track to Whinnyfield Farm. On reaching a junction turn left to retrace our steps into the farmyard, turning right to pass through and onto the lane. Now follow this lane all the way back to the village. As we approach Woodplumpton we pass through a cobbled farmyard and then, a little further, come face to face with a quaint, slightly crooked old cottage. Cuckstool Farm is believed to date from about 1700. It has a corrugated roof which may well sit upon a thatched roof below, in common with a few other houses of similar vintage both on the Fylde and north of the Wyre. Judging from the brickwork and the two-storey section on the left (as seen from the front) there have been additions to the original house. At the main road turn left to the post office and the start.

WALK 17

Around Inskip

A stroll in the countryside around the quiet village of Inskip

Distance:	2¾ miles
Start:	From School Lane, just off the main road through the centre of the village. Grid reference: 464378
Map:	OS Pathfinder 679; OS Landranger 102
Time allowed:	1½ hours
Conditions and difficulties:	Walking boots are likely to be sufficient except after prolonged rain when Wellington boots are preferable
Facilities:	In common with so many villages around the country there is no shop at the time of writing. The Derby Arms is situated less than half a mile south of the village
Public transport:	There is a regular bus service between Preston and Poulton

1 Walk away from the main road towards the farm and follow the lane left, around the corner. As we pass the last house on the right good views open up towards the fells. At the next right-hand corner look out on the left for a large, curious-looking stone, in the shape of a face. They are relics from the former dairy mill that once was situated on Mill Lane. As we pass the next group of houses note the public footpath sign on the left as this is the point to which we shall return later. Where the road bends sharply toward a farm continue straight ahead along a broad track. We are in open countryside now and, over to the left, in a field, can be seen buildings of wartime vintage. They may well be the remnants of the camp that was situated at the village when an airfield occupied the site of what

Communications station near Inskip

– 76 –

Walk 17: Around Inskip

is now the communications station during World War II. The track comes to an end at a gate that leads into a field. Take the gap stile on the left and continue along the left-hand edge of the field to reach a stone stile that brings us into a wood. Go forward to a footbridge on the other side of the narrow wood and cross a broad dyke.

2 Turn left along the left-hand edge of a field, by the side of the dyke. Continue to a stile, left of a gate, and turn right into the next field, towards the corner by the wood. Then follow the wood round to the left, passing a pond in the corner, and at a gate turn right towards a hedge. Keeping the hedge on our right walk away from the wood and, eventually, the side of the field becomes a track. To the right of the fells the low-lying form of the aptly-named and isolated Longridge Fell should be seen. Keep ahead, through a gate, and at the far right-hand corner, just beyond a gate leading to a track on the right, take a stile into the corner of the next field. Follow the hedge to the left as far as the field corner, less than 100 yards away. The legal right of way is a right turn beyond the barbed-wire fence but, in the absence of a stile, this is not a realistic proposition. Therefore, turn right and keep with it to the far corner of the field where gates lead on to a farm track. Ignore the track and the gates but turn left instead and proceed along the right-hand boundary of the adjoining field by the side of a wood.

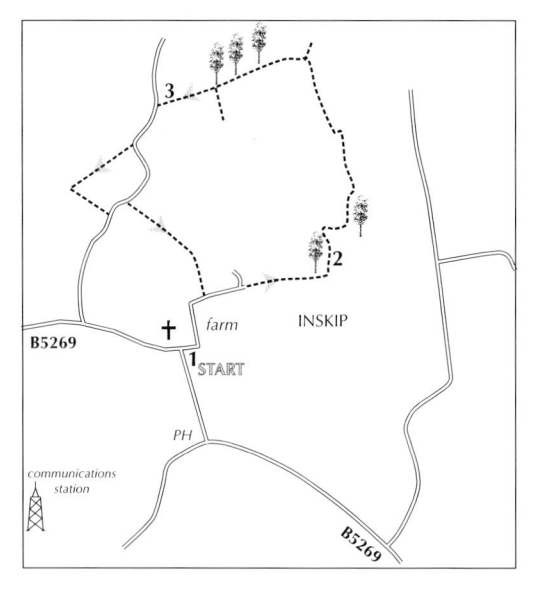

Carry on to the dyke to cross at a footbridge which appears to be resting on the abutment of what was once a more solid structure, suggesting that this may have been a more important track at one time. Now continue along the track which has a hedge on the left and, at the far end of the wood, the track emerges on to an access road by some houses. Over to the left the spire at St Peter's church at Inskip and the masts of the communications station can be seen as we make our way to the far end of the track. They are familiar landmarks on several of the walks.

3 Turn left into the lane and continue around a sharp left-hand bend. Shortly beyond the bend look out for a stile into a field on the right just beyond a house. Proceed along the right-hand edge of the field. Where the right-hand boundary ends carry on to the trees in the far corner. Keeping left of the trees, which surround a pool, take a stile into the next field. Turn left along the field edge and continue with the hedge until reaching a stile to the left of a gate. At the lane ahead we turn

left and, on passing a house that is set back on our left, look for a stile on the right beside a gate into a field.

Once over the stile keep along the right-hand edge of the field. Soon we are joined by a ditch and, at a stile by a copse, cross over, and proceed through the trees passing a picturesque pool before reaching a stile at the far end that leads us into a field. Continue along the right-hand edge but, no more than a few yards further on, another stile on the right takes us across the ditch and into an adjoining field. Turn left along the edge of the field to a stile in the left-hand corner by a gate. Cross over to another stile, a few yards away, in the near right-hand corner of the next field and keep with the right-hand edge. There are three houses ahead and we eventually pass through a narrow enclosed path, between the middle house and the one on the right, to emerge onto a lane. We have rejoined our outward route and all that remains is to turn right and follow the road to the start.

WALK 18

Churchtown

History abounds as we start from one of the oldest churches in the area, encounter an old hall, explore the old market town of Garstang and cross one of the best-known engineering features in the region, the Wyre Aqueduct.

Distance:	7 miles
Start:	From the parish car park adjoining the church. Grid reference: 482428
Maps:	OS Pathfinder 668; OS Landranger 102
Time allowed:	3½ hours
Conditions and difficulties:	Walking boots should be sufficient except after prolonged rain
Facilities:	There is a village shop in Churchtown and various shops and toilet facilities in Garstang
Public transport:	There is a regular bus service from Lancaster and Blackpool

1. From the churchyard walk along Church Street, passing a seventeenth-century barn on the right, Churchgate House with its portico, the Punchbowl Inn with a history going back to the sixteenth century and some pretty eighteenth-century cottages. The market cross at the main junction in the village was erected in the eighteenth century as a dialpost with the sundial at the top of the column. From here walk along Ainspool Lane towards the main road and then turn left as far as the boundary sign at a tributary of the Wyre. Now turn right up the drive leading to Kirkland Hall Farm and cross over the embanked brook again. On approaching the farm, Kirkland Hall appears in the trees to the right. The hall was largely built in the seventeenth and eighteenth centuries and became the property of the Butler family until the late nineteenth century. At the farm buildings the drive swings round to the right to pass the front of the farm and its cottages. The track now bends further round to the right to pass the rear of Kirkland Hall and eventually reaching a stile into a field on the left.

By now we should obtain the first decent views of the Lancashire fells as we follow the right-hand boundary of the field to a corner facing a pool. Turn left with the field boundary until reaching a gate. Continue in the same direction, ignoring the track to the right. A panoramic view of the fells has now opened up from Beacon Fell and Parlick on the right to Calder Fell and Grizedale Fell on the left. Eventually, at a gate, the track becomes made-up as we turn right to pass a wood and on through a farmyard, continuing in the same direction, until reaching the A6 trunk road.

Turn left alongside the front of Cross House Farm but before reaching the Garstang boundary sign take a gate in the hedge across the main road and carefully negotiate the steep slope down to the stile and footbridge. Now go forward half-left to join the river Wyre which, at this stage of its journey from the fells to the Irish Sea, has lost its fresh youthfulness but has yet to acquire the slow and stately properties of the mature river it becomes a few miles to the west. Soon we catch a first glimpse of the stylish arch of the fine aqueduct that carries the Lancaster Canal over the river Wyre. We too shall cross this structure but, for now, we continue forward to a footbridge and on, in the same direction, to a kissing gate. The next gate can be seen ahead and, from there, maintain the same general direction but rise slightly across the sloping ground to reach a wicket gate by the side of the canal.

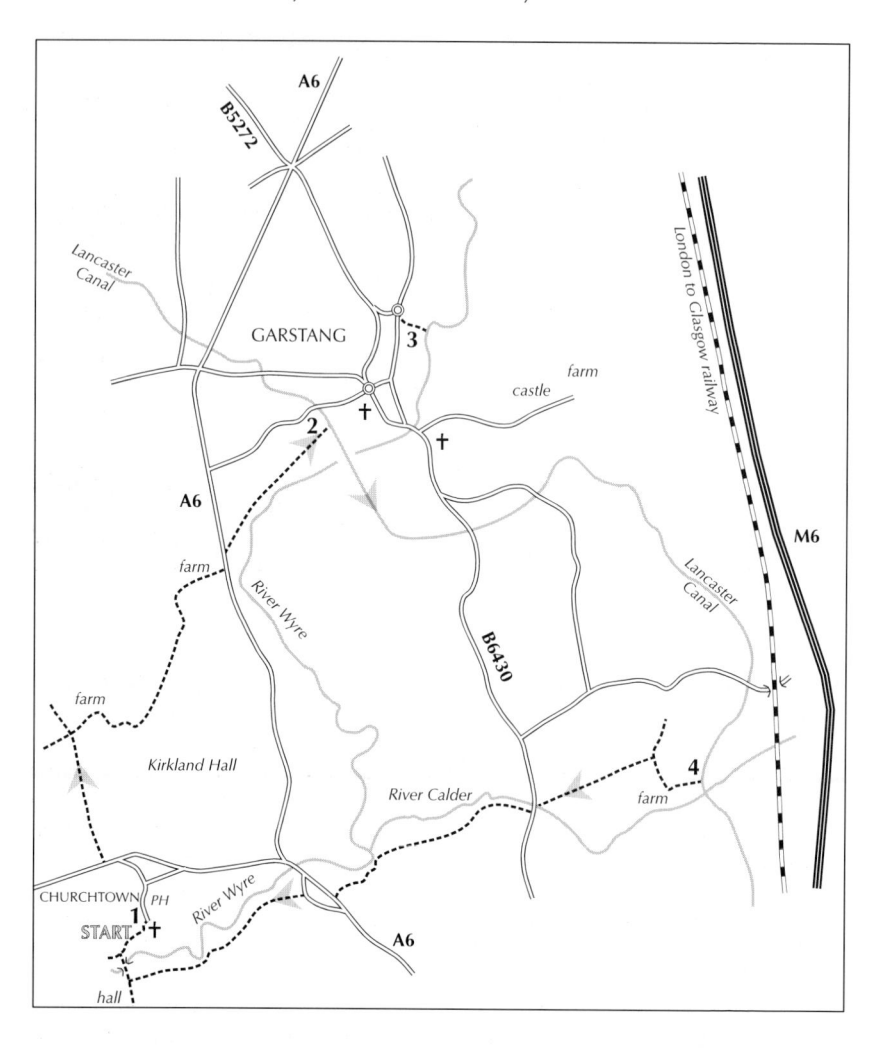

2 We shall cross the aqueduct later but, for now, turn left and pass the marina on the right alongside Th' 'Owd Tithe Barn which pre-dates the canal. At the bridge (no.62) take the path to the left to gain the road and cross over the canal via the footbridge.

Pass St Thomas Parish Hall on the right and the quaint School Cottages on

Walk 18: Churchtown

Old Cottage, Garstang

the left before reaching the parish church of St Thomas, Garstang, with its stocky tower. It was erected in 1770 prior to which time St Helen's at Churchtown was the principal church for Garstang. At the road junction cross over the mini roundabout into Church Street. Use the pedestrian access on the right to cross the road and, at the far end of Church Street by the Market Cross, stands the Royal Oak Hotel with its cobbled courtyard. The present market cross dates from 1752 and replaced an earlier cross. It is, in fact, a column with a ball at the top, similar to those at Churchtown and Poulton. Markets have been held here since early in the fourteenth century and the High Street still has a medieval feel to it. Situated between Preston and Lancaster the town was an important centre during the era of stage coaches. Horses were changed here and there were several coaching inns of which the Royal Oak Hotel was the most prominent. Its visitors included Sir Walter Scott. At the far side of the Market Place is the eighteenth-century town hall and, to the left of it, the Market Hall. Opposite the town hall is another coaching inn, the Eagle and Child, the name being associated with the Earl of Derby's coat of arms.

As we make our way up High Street note the narrow passages that connect the main street with what was then the back road. These are known as weinds and are believed to have had a defensive purpose, giving a measure of protection in times of invasion from the Scots. There are some eighteenth-century cottages here including no.43 with a datestone of 1744. A hundred years earlier troops occupied houses along this street during the Civil War and, at the time of the Jacobite rebellions of 1715 and 1745, more troops arrived to occupy the town. At the next roundabout turn right to the car park but note the Arts Centre beyond the roundabout. It was the former Grammar School, built in 1756. To the left of the car park entrance is the Discovery Centre which provides useful information about the surrounding countryside and the town itself. There are toilet facilities in the car park and it is worth the extra few yards to look upon the Wyre as it bends sharply round a sandy bluff.

3 Now we must re-trace our steps, turning left at the entrance to the car park and taking the right fork before the Royal Oak Hotel. Continue over the mini roundabout to the canal bridge and head south along the towpath to cross the Wyre Aqueduct, designed by John Rennie in 1797. A little further on we pass a milepost indicating that it is 13 miles to Lancaster and 17 miles to Preston. At this point we are less than a mile south of the centre of Garstang and, having passed under bridge 60, we approach bridge 59 that carries the main road into the town. The path has now changed course from a south-easterly direction to face the north east but only for a short while. Beyond bridge 58 look across the canal to the left for a glimpse of the scant remains of Greenhalgh Castle dating from 1490 and built for Thomas Stanley, the Earl of Derby. The castle was taken by Cromwell's forces during the Civil War and, in time, fell into ruins.

Shortly the canal veers round to the right and under bridge 57 to pursue a south-easterly course. Beyond bridge 55 the West Coast Main Line draws alongside the canal but only briefly as the canal now changes direction again, this time to the south-west, under bridge 54 and passing industrial units on the other side. Another small canal basin is passed before reaching bridge 53 from where we need to head westwards. Just beyond the bridge take the path up to the right leading onto a track but before doing so note a second modest aqueduct a few yards ahead that carries the canal over the river Calder.

4 Having reached the track that crosses over the bridge turn left to eventually reach a row of terraced farm cottages. Here, turn right along another track, to a point where it bends a little to the right. Look out for a stile on the left (there is no footpath sign) and cross over into a field, walking along its boundary with a hedge on our right. We now follow an unwavering straight line through a series of fields towards the B6430 at Catterall. At the end of the final field we make our way via a stile up to the road and then turn left for a few yards only, sufficient to cross the river Calder, before turning right along the path that runs alongside the river. A large recreation ground lies to our left but at its far end we need to rise up to an embankment and follow the river to its confluence with the larger Wyre. Just beyond this junction the path leaves the river and stumbles upon waste ground where the going looks uncertain but a track is quickly joined and followed round to the left to join an industrial road. Turn right up this road until it meets the A6 again.

Now turn right along the main road until we reach the bridge taking the A6 over the river Wyre. Don't cross the bridge but turn back to the left along Old Lancaster Road. Less than 100 yards along this road a farm drive will be found on the right. Turn through the gate and along the track. Beyond a stile we draw level with a crook in the river where St Helen's church tower should be visible once again. Continue to the buildings ahead of us. On reaching a junction of tracks turn right beside the cattle grid, along the drive to Catterall Hall. Just as the drive bends to the left take a stile on the bend and cross to the suspension bridge over the river. On the other side follow a banked track round to the right

Walk 18: Churchtown

Suspension Bridge across the Wyre at Churchtown

towards the back of the church. Arguably the most historic church on the Fylde, its oldest parts are twelfth-century pillars in the north aisle but there are elements within the building from all the subsequent centuries. Other highlights include the fifteenth-century tower with stone turret at the top of the staircase, a Norman font and the fifteenth-century misericords in the rear choir stalls. There is a curious structure at the north-east corner of the church which has the appearance of a small house and it has been suggested that this was used as lodgings by the monks of Cockersands Abbey when they called there. The graveyard contains the graves of rebels who joined the Jacobites in 1715, an episode that caused the Butler family to lose their home at Rawcliffe Hall.

WALK 19

Great and Little Eccleston

A stroll along the banks of the Wyre and a return through undulating fields. On the way we encounter what may be the last toll bridge in Lancashire and one of the few remaining in the North of England.

Distance:	4 miles
Start:	From the market square, adjacent to the junction of Leckonby Street and High Street, in the centre of the village. Grid reference: 427402
Map:	OS Pathfinder 668/679; OS Landranger 102
Time allowed:	2 hours
Conditions and difficulties:	Walking boots are likely to be sufficient except after periods of prolonged rain when Wellington boots are recommended
Facilities:	The White Bull and Black Bull are situated across the High Street from each other. There is a range of shops including the Post Office on the High Street and public toilets are situated at the beginning of the journey
Public transport:	There is a regular bus service from Preston, Blackpool and Lancaster

1 From the market square (once the venue for a large annual fair) in the centre of the village, next to the junction of Leckonby Street and High Street, cross the road to the White Bull and turn left opposite the Black Bull. Public toilets are signposted down this side street along which we proceed to reach a junction of tracks. Turn right along Back Lane (a remnant of the medieval layout of the village) until it reaches a small estate of modern houses. Turn left to locate a drive leading down to the by-pass.

Cross over the busy main road to a stile opposite and slightly to the right, next to a gate. Advance just a few yards to another stile on the right and then head away, half-left, across the large field to the far left-hand corner. Here a stile leads us along the right-hand edge of the next field to a stile at the foot of the Wyre embankment. Steps lead up to the top of the bank where we turn left to follow the river.

2 The man-made embankment is a reminder of the vulnerability of the surrounding land to flooding in the past. Nowadays, however, water levels are closely monitored and controlled. From the bank there are unimpeded views of the Lancashire fells. Eventually we encounter a footbridge across the river but the waymark sign should be ignored as we remain on the south side of the Wyre, passing a bridge that carries a pipeline over the river. Now continue round to the left and onwards, drawing nearer to the caravan site at Little Eccleston ahead. Eventually a ladder stile is crossed just as the river begins to bend to the right to pass under Cartford Bridge. Ignore a second ladder stile in a hedge on the left

– 84 –

Walk 19: Great and Little Eccleston

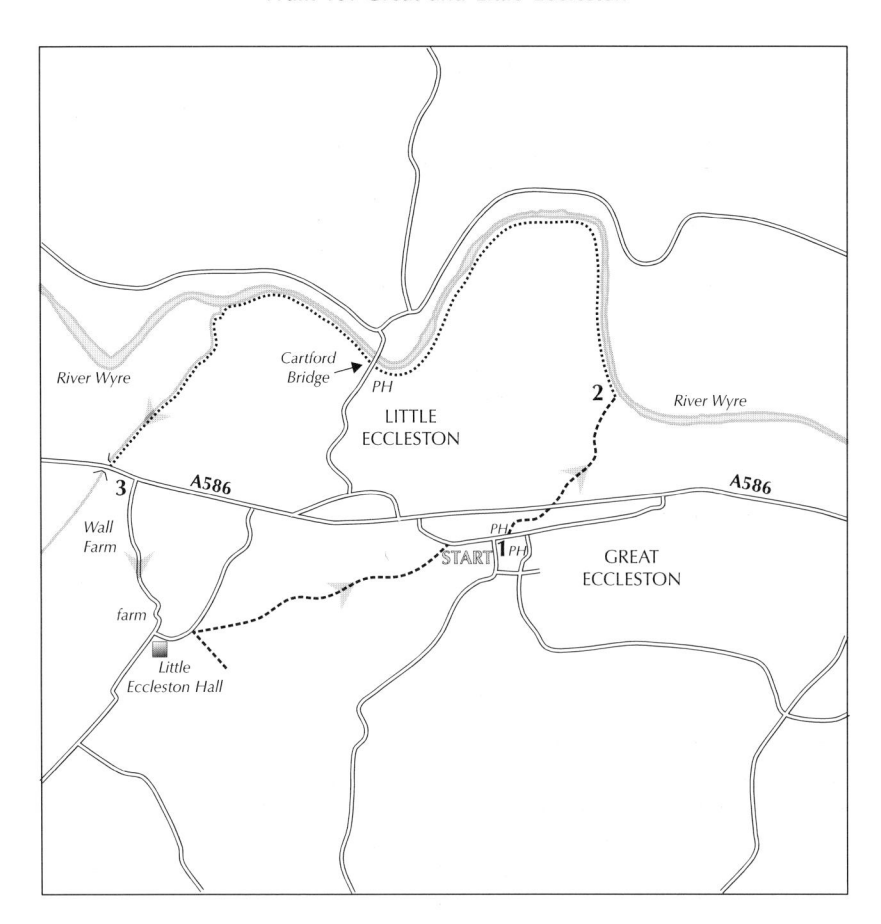

and follow the riverside path alongside Cartford Hotel (believed to be haunted) to emerge onto a lane beside Cartford Bridge where tolls are charged. The present bridge replaces a wooden predecessor.

Our route is straight across the lane and over a ladder stile but it is worth the short walk up the hill through Little Eccleston, by way of a small diversion. Continue alongside the Wyre with a caravan site on the left and Cartford Bridge toll house on our right. At the far end of the caravan site we pass through a kissing gate and out into the open along the embankment. At the next stile, which is some distance away, we leave the Wyre and follow a minor tributary, Thistleton Brook, to the left. Continue by the side of this brook all the way to Wallpool Bridge where a ladder stile takes us up to the A586 that crosses the bridge.

3 Turn left along a pavement, by the side of the road, as we pass from the Larbreck boundary into Little Eccleston. We need tolerate the traffic for a brief spell only as our route is along the first lane to the right. This is Wall Lane, a quiet but narrow lane along which care is required in order to listen out for approaching vehicles. Children should be closely supervised along this section. Note, first of

Back Lane, Great Eccleston, remnant of medieval layout

Walk 19: Great and Little Eccleston

all, Wall Farm on the right, the quaint cottage with mullioned windows in the gable and a deep porch. It is one of the oldest buildings in this area with parts dating back to the fifteenth century. Keep along this quiet by-way which meanders round to the right and to the left as we pass a farm to reach a junction with Little Eccleston Hall in front of us. Bearing a datestone of 1638 it has been added to since. It was once owned by the Ffrance family, who later became the squires of Rawcliffe. Turn left here and continue until we pass the last house on the right. A public footpath sign points in two directions across the field on the right. Negotiating the stile, we need to aim half-left to the far left-hand corner of the field. As we make a gradual, diagonal descent through the field, look out for Copp church tower and the wireless station at Inskip ahead while, over to the right, the spire of Elswick church is visible briefly.

From the stile at the corner of the field cross into the next field and, once again, we need to aim for the far left-hand diagonal corner where another stile needs to be negotiated close to a brook. Now continue along the right-hand boundary of the field to a further stile at the beginning of an attractive, broad grassy path. This section is, alas, all too brief as we return, via a stile, into an open field. Follow the right-hand edge alongside a brook, bordered by trees, until resuming our journey along another enclosed path beyond the next stile. The brook continues alongside us but soon this rustic scene comes to an end as the path becomes made-up and we enter the outskirts of Great Eccleston once again. At the main village road turn right along West End and back to the centre immediately noting the single-storey former smithy and, further on, the Old Chapel with its date stone of 1870 and the low single-storey building used as a restaurant but thought to have a long history. There is, indeed, a good variety of housing styles, sizes and ages along West End as we return to the start.

WALK 20

Pilling and Eagland Hill

Discover the mossland of Over Wyre

Distance:	10 miles
Start:	The car park, diagonally opposite from Pilling Pottery in the centre of the village, along School Lane. Grid reference: 403482
Maps:	OS Pathfinder 668; OS Landranger 102
Time allowed:	5 hours
Conditions and difficulties:	Walking boots should be sufficient except after prolonged rain. Avoid windy or wet days as much of this route is exposed with little shelter
Facilities:	There are public toilets at the car park and two public houses that are passed en route. There are also shops and a payphone in the village centre
Public transport:	Pilling is served by a regular bus service from Fleetwood and Lancaster

1 Turn right from the car park and walk up to the Olde Ship inn to locate a public footpath on the right. The path is enclosed and narrow until we reach a ladder stile. Just beyond the stile note the pinfold on the right, built on the site of the original. It was used to impound stray animals, mainly in the days before enclosures of farmland, and the owner of the stray cattle or pigs would have to pay to recover his animals. Beyond the pinfold the way ahead opens up and we continue until, past a barn, a left turn is taken along a track which veers to the right as it passes another barn. Continue to a gate with a pedestrian gate to its left and, having passed through, veer half-left initially along a concrete path parallel to the hedge on our left. At the far end of the field is a footbridge from where Damside Mill can be seen over to the left. Now go straight ahead, passing by the side of the meandering Pilling Water until crossing it at a footbridge ahead. From here aim diagonally to the left towards a group of trees beyond a hedge. On reaching the hedge continue with it on the left, passing the derelict Field House, a traditional Pilling cottage with a corrugated roof. At the far left-hand corner we leave the field at a stile to the right of a gate and proceed to the Lancaster road.

Turn left for a few yards but, at the house opposite, cross over and enter its garden to locate a stile in the far right-hand corner. From the stile follow the right-hand boundary of the field to the corner where a footbridge will be seen. Cross this and then another bridge leading us to a pleasant enclosed and grassy path beside a brook on the right and a narrow copse on the left. At the far end there is a choice of stiles. Take the one on the left and proceed along the right-hand boundary of the field. There is a ditch on the right and this turns right at another copse. Look out for a stile here from where we continue along a grassy path, enclosed as far as the next stile. Keep along the right-hand field boundary

Walk 20: Pilling and Eagland Hill

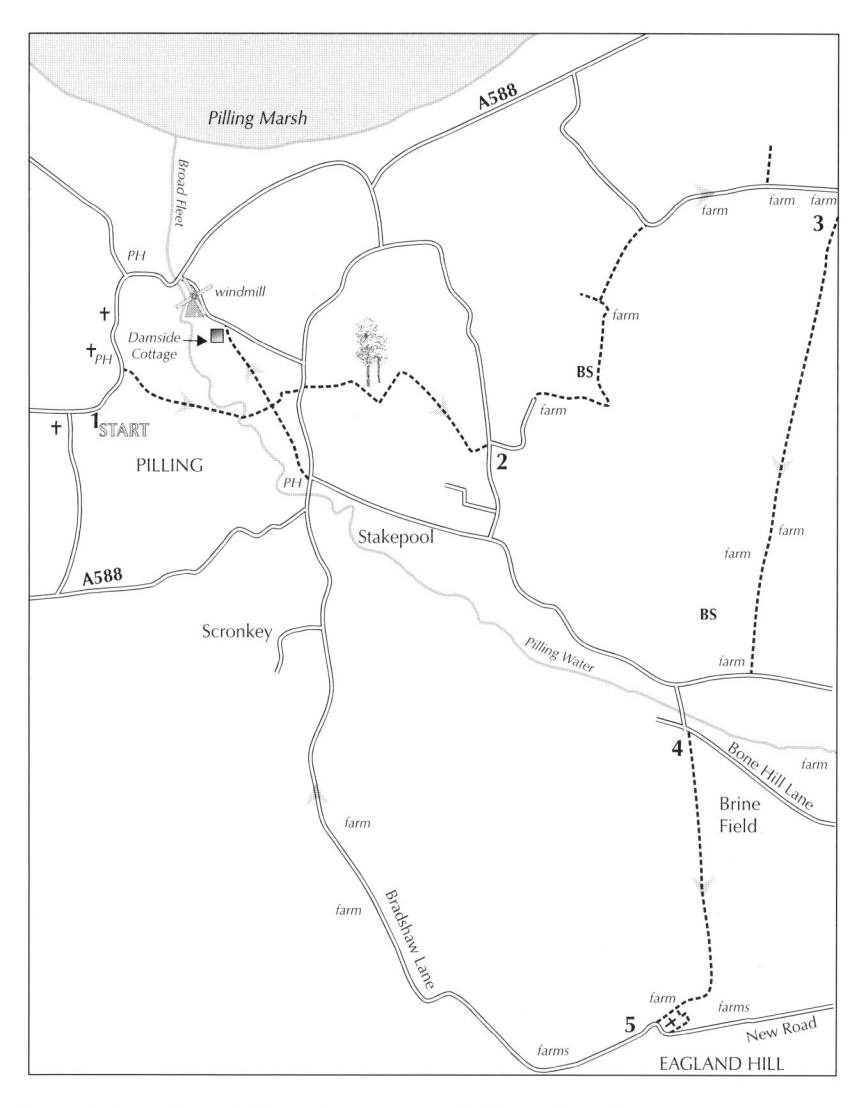

beyond this stile and through a series of fields until reaching a stile leading to the right at a field corner. Ignore this but, instead, continue round to the left to vacate the field at a stile by a gate and out onto a country lane at a junction.

2 Walk up the lane ahead of us and note Moss Side Cottage on the right with its corrugated roof and built-in garage, converted probably from a shippon that once formed part of many of the older traditional houses. Keep with the lane as it swings round to the left towards Bonds Farm and notice how the field butts on to the road with no physical separation such as a fence or hedge. Indeed, looking eastwards across the flat land towards the fells it is plain to see that there is very little in the way of hedges or fences, giving a rare glimpse of what the English

landscape must have looked like before the enclosure movement of the eighteenth century. Pass in front of Bonds Farm and look out for a ditch on the right beyond the last main farm building. Immediately after the ditch turn right and proceed alongside the watercourse into a field until the far end where a footbridge is crossed.

Turn left here and follow the field edge, through a gate, to continue in the same direction along a track. Just as this track bends to the right look through the hedge on the left and note the tall boundary stone. On the right there are splendid unimpeded views available on a clear day of the Lancashire fells, from Beacon Fell in the south to the area of Ward's Stone in the north. The track passes another farm and then turns sharply to the left and right before straightening out to meet the relatively quiet Gulf Lane. Turn right here and follow the lane round the corner. Eventually we pass Near Moss Farm and then, just beyond a track and bridleway on the left, Moss House Farm. The names confirm, if proof is needed, that we are well and truly traversing mossland scenery. At the next farm, Moss Edge Farm, turn right, directly through the farmyard, and out by a gate at the far side onto what is initially a concrete track.

3 This track, dead straight for over a mile, now takes us in a roughly southerly direction across Cockerham Moss – flat, desolate at times, and often windswept but yet distinctive in its own way. Continuing along the second half of this long straight stretch we have the benefit of a hedge on our left. Between the gaps in this hedge can be seen the woodlands that now colonise parts of Cockerham Moss and, immediately to its south, Winmarleigh Moss. Just beyond Poplar Farm on the left and Poplar Grove the track bends very slightly to the left at Crawley's Dyke. A public footpath follows the dyke on our left into the wilderness of Winmarleigh Moss while, on the right but not visible, is Crawley's Cross, a well-known boundary stone by the side of the dyke. Our way is forward however and as the hedges, that have enclosed the track for some distance, come to an end look through the gaps to the left and right and try and imagine trains passing. It may be difficult to visualize but this is where the course of the Garstang–Pilling railway crossed. There are concrete posts, almost certainly erected by the railway (as they are similar to those at other crossing points), to which were attached the gates to guard the crossing. While looking left note the raised mound about a quarter of a mile away upon which stands Cogie Hill Farm. Similar mounds supporting farms or larger communities are a feature of this area. They provided some protection from flooding before the mosses were drained and names such as Island Farm give a clear idea as to what the scenery must have looked like at one time. Passing through the yard of Crawley's Cross Farm we emerge onto the Pilling–Garstang road.

We need to turn right here but, before doing so, look straight ahead at another farm on a raised mound. This is Bone Hill Farm with a sinister past for, during the eighteenth and into the nineteenth centuries, a notorious family here were engaged in running a 'Baby Farm' where unwanted offsprings of a daughter or mistress of wealthy individuals were disposed of. The area was also known for cockfighting which continued until the end of the nineteenth century despite the banning of such exhibitions by the Prevention of Cruelty to Animals Act in 1849. Care is required along this road as it can be busy and, to make things worse,

Walk 20: Pilling and Eagland Hill

Farms on the Moss

there is little verge as the sides drop down quite steeply. However, it is only a short distance before we take the first left turn into Bone Hill Lane, just beyond the Pilling boundary, and cross over Pilling Water once again before reaching a junction. As Bone Hill Lane bends to the left a kissing gate will be seen ahead, to the left of a field gate.

4 From the kissing gate walk away alongside a dyke next to the field edge. The extensive system of dykes is another feature of this mossland and it is worth contemplating that this walk would have been impossible to undertake until the nineteenth century when landowners such as Thomas Ffrance of Rawcliffe Hall drained and reclaimed large tracts of land. Note the pipes that dip underground to the left. They are part of the infrastructure of the brine wells that extend from Preesall to the Eagland Hill area which lies ahead of us, beyond the trees. On meeting a dyke on the left cross the stile into a field that is noticeably higher than the previous one (perhaps the underlying peat has not been removed). Continue in the same direction across the next field and, at the far side, cross a footbridge. Looking left at this point, along the dyke, the eye leads directly to Parlick while over to our right it should be possible to see the spire of Pilling Church to the left of a group of trees. In this land of flat, hedgeless fields it makes a pleasant change to walk alongside a hedge again and gain a measure of protection from any north-east winds. Continue to the next footbridge and through the next field, alongside the hedge. Having surmounted another stile continue ahead, ignoring the stile on the left.

On reaching a gateway at the next field corner, having just passed under wires, turn right without going through the gate so that a hedge is on our left. We are

Fylde Coast and Country Walks

The fells from Eagland Hill

Walk 20: Pilling and Eagland Hill

now heading directly towards Eagland Hill. We pass a pond on our left and in the far left-hand corner of the field cross over a stile and onto a grassy track with farm buildings over to our right. We soon arrive at a small square, presumably the centre of this compact hamlet, with the low church on our left. Turn left here to face the church and note the Victorian post box set into a wall. Go left again to locate a gate and follow the path round the other side of St Mark's Church to leave at the church gates. The track now passes some cotttages on the right and some modern property before emerging onto the lane that skirts around the edge of the hamlet. We need to turn right here but it is worth a brief look around this farming hamlet occupying another of the prominent mounds mentioned earlier.

5 Leaving Eagland Hill we turn into Bradshaw Lane and, initially, pursue a course well above the surrounding moss. Before long we encounter farms on either side of the road and then the lane bends to the right, in a north-westerly direction towards Pilling. For much of the first mile this road is straight except for a double bend. During the winter months in particular there is a lot of bird activity in the area with large numbers of pink-footed geese, for example, present in the fields around Eagland Hill and Pilling. Look out too for a variety of farmland birds that can often be seen around the small copse on the right, beyond the second bend. On passing a couple of farms the road begins to widen and meander more before reaching a junction with a busier road close to the hamlet of Scronkey, a little to the left. In just a further half mile we arrive at Stakepool where there is a junction with the A588 Lancaster road. Continue ahead to another junction with the Garstang road on the right. On the left at this point is the Elletson Arms recalling the family of landowners who owned Parrox Hall near Knott End.

Now cross over and advance towards the end of the pub car park where a public footpath will be seen leading into a field beside a small wood. From here go half-right towards a hedge and find a gate leading into the next field. Now there is a choice between veering half-left to a footbridge and then retracing our steps back to the car park or pressing ahead, across the field, aiming to the left of a small copse to reach a gap in the fence, to the right of a hedge. Pass through the gap and head half-left across the field towards the windmill and, as long as we maintain a line towards Damside Mill, we should arrive unerringly at a kissing gate from where we must continue along the left-hand edge of a small field to reach another kissing gate. Now proceed along a pleasant narrow, enclosed, grassy path leading to a road but, as we do so, note Damside Cottage on our left, believed to date from the late sixteenth or early seventeenth century. Once through the kissing gate we must now turn left along the road where there are other old cottages and, of course, the windmill, built in 1808 by Ralph Slater and now in use as a private residence. Now follow the instructions in Walk 23 (Pilling Marsh) under section 4 while returning to the starting point in the village.

WALK 21

Stalmine

A pleasant venture, mainly along quiet country lanes, that offers much of interest including some of the finest panoramic views in this part of Lancashire as well as a slice of history.

Distance:	6 miles
Start:	Along Smithy Lane that runs west from the A588 in the centre of the village, at the top of the hill. Grid reference: 374454
Map:	OS Pathfinder 658; OS Landranger 102
Time allowed:	3 hours
Conditions and difficulties:	Walking boots should be sufficient except after prolonged rain.
Facilities:	There are public houses at Stalmine and Wardleys and a village shop in Stalmine
Public transport:	There are bus services from Blackpool, Fleetwood and Lancaster

1 Walk down Smithy Lane, past Headsway Cottage on the right and Carr End Lane on the left. Note another road on the left, just a little further, as we shall return along the track that can be seen at this junction. For now, though, we follow Grange Lane round to the right and soon emerge into open countryside. The chimney at the Hillhouse industrial complex near Thornton can be seen to the left and, indeed, re-appears at different points along the walk. As we progress to a left-hand bend, the brightly coloured buildings at Freeport should also be visible, on the horizon ahead. Over to the right Preesall and its former windmill can be seen occupying the higher ground, a modest hill known as a drumlin, formed at the end of the Ice Age when the glaciers retreated.

The road bends to the right and then, a little further on, to the left. Immediately before the left-hand bend and the farm buildings take a grassy path off to the right. It is broad with a ditch on the right and bounded by hedges. The path passes a pond on the right before swinging to the left. The track, which can be very wet at times, later narrows towards a road where we turn right, briefly, before taking the first left turn along a made-up road signposted as a bridleway.

2 We pass a small farm and a scrapyard on our right while, a little further on, note the iron boundary marker on the left by a ditch. Continuing along this track a view should be obtained of the Pharos Lighthouse at Fleetwood by looking half-right. We are now on the Preesall Brine Field where a sign lists the number of wells in the area. The brine pumps are the remnants of a much larger operation of salt extraction with a salt works and mineral line but regular flooding of the mines led to the closure of the salt works. Continue along Corcas Lane (which follows the route of the brine pipeline that runs between Preesall and Burn Naze across the river) until it arrives at a junction with the Wyre Way at Heads.

We must turn left here along a made-up lane, passing a caravan site on the right. We soon reach a left-hand bend with an embankment on the right-hand

– 94 –

Walk 21: Stalmine

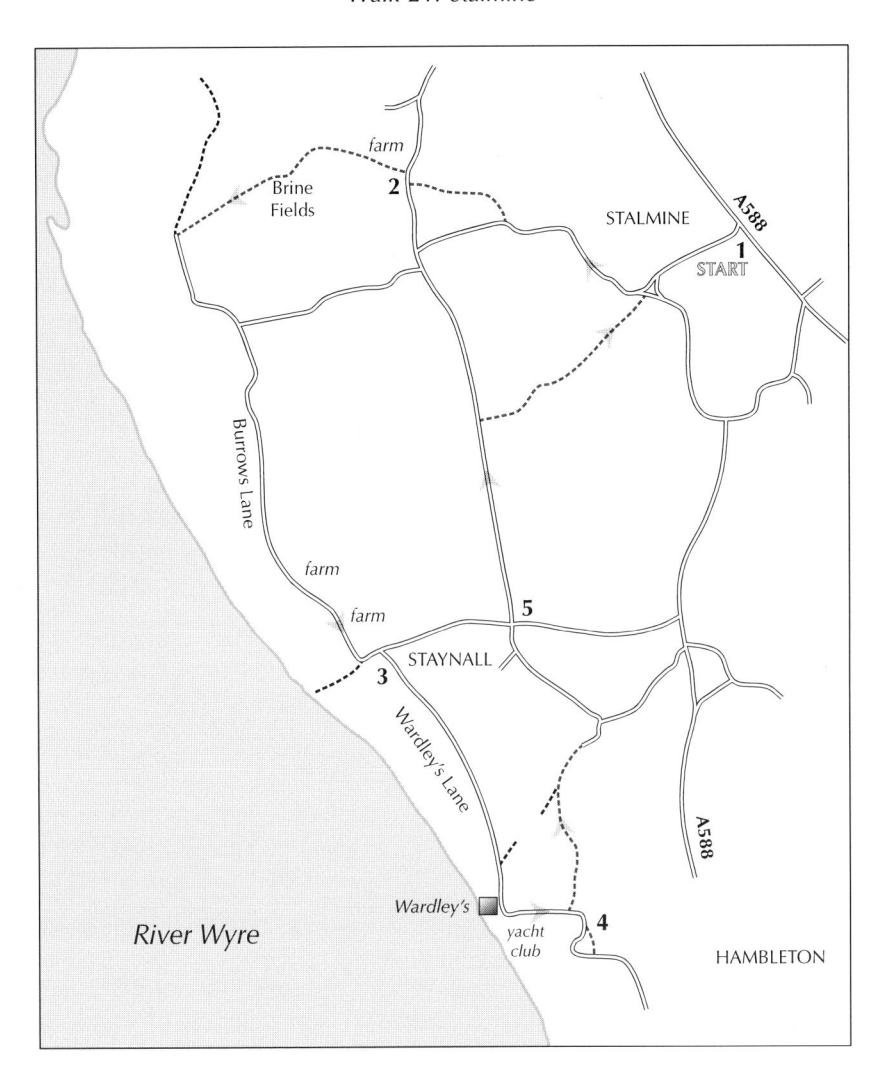

side. Climb onto the embankment, designed to protect the low-lying land from flooding, for a better view across the Burrows Marsh Nature Reserve and the Wyre. Note also the straight line of debris that has been stranded at the highest tides. At the road junction with Highgate Lane follow the embankment to the right, above Burrows Lane, but, where the road and the embankment part company, return to the road which begins a steady climb to provide us with good views across the marshes between the gaps in the hedge. Marsh Mill can be seen across the river in Thornton and, when we reach the top of the hill there are superb panoramic views over the Wyre towards Fleetwood, to the fells in the east and, on a clear day, the Lake District mountains. Now the lane begins to lose height as we pass Burrows Farm. Further gaps in the hedge will reveal views of the country park at Stanah, ahead and to the right. We pass Carter's Farm and eventually follow the lane round to the left at a corner and then take first right in the farming community of Staynall. If a quicker return to Stalmine is required ignore the right-hand turn in the village but continue to crossroads, turn left, and follow the directions at 5 below.

3 We are now on Wardley's Lane and, at first, there are fine views once again towards the fells before we drop below the hedge line. Meanwhile the vista on the right eventually opens up as we pass under the wires and see the Wyre meandering from Skippool. The lane now drops past a caravan site and the inn at Wardley's, a place of historic interest. This was once a port of local importance where sailing ships brought flax from Russia for Kirkham's linen industry and timber from North America. Ships of upto 300 tons could be accommodated until Fleetwood replaced it in the 1840s as a port. From the car park of this inn look across the river at low tide and the wooden base supports for the old landing stages can be seen. A little further at the corner we come to Wardley's Pool, home to the Wardley Marine Yacht Club. Follow the road round and just before a right-hand bend note a public footpath on the left, down which we shall walk in a little while. A few yards further on round the bend another path leaves the road at a stile; we shall begin our return journey along this path shortly. Keep along the lane, by the side of the creeks, until, leaving them behind, we turn left to follow the road inland but for less than one hundred yards as we part company with the road at a stile in the hedge on the left. As we cross the stile note the bungalow ahead, across the field, as we need to aim to the left of it. A stile to the right of a gate leads us back onto the road at the creeks.

4 Turn right along the road, but only briefly, as we take the first public footpath on the right. The track leads, initially, to the rear of a bungalow but do not enter the grounds of this property. Instead, follow the grassy path by a ditch to the left of the private grounds. Stiles are encountered in quick succession bringing us out onto a field. Proceed along the left-hand edge before reaching a bend and take another stile on our left leading us, via a footbridge, into a field. Now follow the right-hand boundary and, as we round the bend in the field, a stile will be seen that leads us onto an enclosed green way. We pass under power cables and, a little further on, ignore the footbridge and public footpath on the left. Soon the track enters a corner of a field and we continue along the left-hand edge to vacate it at gates leading us onto a track which joins an access road to some houses. Now head away from the houses along this access road until it reaches a junction with a lane. Turn left here to eventually pass New Road and, further on, reach crossroads. Situated on the hill to the left is the hamlet of Staynall.

5 From the crossroads proceed straight ahead up Highgate Lane. As we progress along this lane a stile will be seen on the left, just beyond a house on the right. The public footpath (which we ignore) seems to head directly up to Burrows Farm on the ridge but, in fact, it leads to Staynall. We remain on the road that straightens out towards High Gate Farm ahead but then, just as the road curves gently to the right, take a stile on the right (to the left of a gate) and proceed along the left-hand edge of the field. On the horizon to the left one can see Preesall windmill again. At the far left-hand corner two stiles are encountered in

Walk 21: Stalmine

Headsway Cottage, Stalmine

quick succession that lead us into the next field. Proceed in the same direction, along the left-hand edge, to pass two ponds, one behind the hedge on our left and the other immediately to our right. Near the far left-hand corner of the field climb the ladder stile on the left that deposits us onto a farm track.

Turn right along the track but for just a few yards before crossing over a stile on the left from where we proceed along an enclosed green path that develops into a track before finally emerging onto a driveway at the edge of Stalmine. Note the houses on the right bearing datestones of 1703 and 1684 as we follow the drive to the junction that we encountered at the beginning of the walk. Advance just a few yards and then turn right where Grange Road becomes Smithy Lane. Pass Headsway Cottage, on the left, again and the terraces of small nineteenth-century cottages on the right before returning to the start. The variety of houses and the range of their ages help to give an impression of a village that has evolved gradually and adapted to changing times while revealing aspects of its past.

WALK 22

Knott End-on-Sea

A choice of walks, offering fine views across the bay or a visit to the pretty village of Preesall, via the brine fields. Binoculars would be useful.

Distance:	4½ or 7 miles
Start:	From the car park close to the slipway at the edge of the River Wyre opposite Fleetwood. Grid reference: 346485
Maps:	OS Pathfinder 658; OS Landranger 102
Time allowed:	Via Preesall: 2½ hours.
	Via the embankment: 3½ hours
Conditions and difficulties:	Walking boots should be sufficient
Facilities:	There are public toilets at the car park and the usual range of facilities associated with a small town
Public transport:	There are bus services to Knott End from Blackpool, Fleetwood and Lancaster

1 From the car park that occupies the site of the former Knott End terminus of the branch line from Garstang, take the riverside path and walk upstream, passing Knott End Golf Club. Across the river are the landing stages and, beyond, the Pharos Lighthouse and Queen's Terrace. To the right is the Lower Lighthouse. On reaching Sea Dyke Cottage turn left in front of the cottage. The track cuts across the golf course but we don't; instead, at the first opportunity, turn sharp right beside the cottages to follow a track that soon becomes grassy as it runs along the right-hand side of the golf course at the river's edge. The path briefly becomes gravelly and rises above fishermens' cottages on the riverside. Ahead and slightly left in the trees are farm buildings and we now need to head across the golf course in that direction, taking care as we do so. Before crossing note the colourful buildings of the Freeport complex across the river, together with the adjacent docks. A track is reached on the other side of the golf course leading down to a farm. Our route swings to the left, in front of a gateway, to pass Hackensall Hall, which though dated 1656 is mainly nineteenth century when the hall was rebuilt for Richard Fleetwood of Rossall. Beyond the hall there is a choice of routes. If wishing to walk across the brine fields to Preesall follow the instructions from 5 below but otherwise continue as directed under 2 below.

2 Now proceed, straight ahead, ignoring the path to the left. Eventually we pass an access track to a farm on the right but, again, we continue ahead until reaching another track. This is straight and bears the hallmarks of a former railway line. Indeed it was the former branch line from Garstang to Knott End but this section was closed as long ago as 1950. Cross over and forge ahead, following the track as it curves right to run parallel with the former railway. After some time the track crosses the ditch on our left but, before doing so, look half-right for a

Walk 22: Knott End-on-Sea

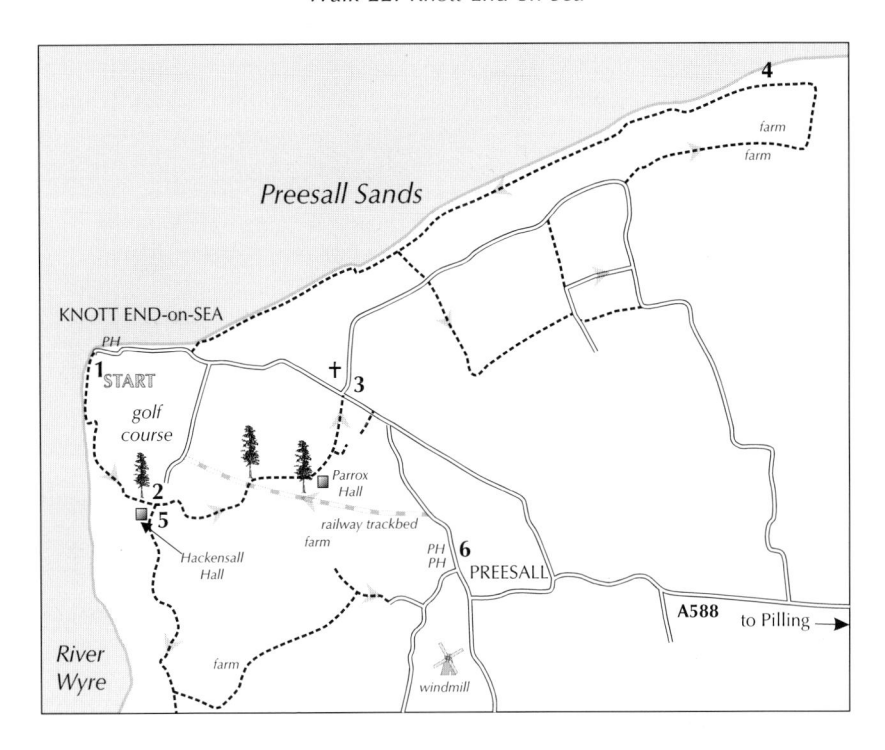

glimpse of Preesall Mill. Now we are heading towards the left-hand edge of woodland and, set in this woodland, is Parrox Hall, another hall with a long history. The present building dates from the late sixteenth century when acquired by the Butler family. It later passed into the hands of the Elletsons through marriage. Just as we begin to pass the wood on our right look out for a stile on the left. Cross over so that we are heading away from the woodland and through a small conifer plantation towards St Oswald Church. The path leads to another stile in a fence and then, a few yards further on, veer right, aiming for a cross – the War Memorial. Pass by the side of the memorial to find a gate leading to a road.

3 Our way is straight ahead onto Pilling Lane but note that there are public toilets about 100 yards along the path on our left before crossing the road. At the right-hand bend follow Pilling Lane and note that, although much of the housing stock stands on surplus farmland, the former farmhouses can still be seen amongst them. Ignore the public footpath sign on the right but, at Sandy Bay Caravan Park on the left, there is a public footpath sign to the left and to the right. If a shorter route back to the start is required turn left to the embankment and left again to Knott End but otherwise turn right and head away over the stile in a straight line alongside a ditch and cross a second stile. Over to the left in the distance are the fells with the spire of Pilling Church discernible in front of these hills. Beyond a third stile a footbridge is passed on the right and then a second footbridge over which we cross. Now turn immediately left to follow another ditch and continue to a stile and then on to another stile, left of a gate, leading

The Black Bull, Preesall

on to a narrow made-up road known as Tongues Lane. Turn left and follow this road round to the right, passing extensive game hatcheries, mainly ducks and pheasants, to reach Pilling Lane once again at a T-junction. Turn left and continue until reaching a left-hand corner.

On the right is a bridleway and we now need to turn right along this track. Pass Cocker Dyke House (note the black-and-white building with mullioned windows) and one or two windswept residences before the track enters a field and approaches a farm. Our route skirts round to the left of the farm to join a more formal track on the other side. We soon encounter a second farm, passing an old farmhouse on the left with external steps leading up to a first floor storage area. The track now turns left and we are heading towards the embankment. On our right, in the trees, is Fluke Hall. When the track bends sharply to the right take the public footpath to the left, along the left-hand side of the field beside a hedge. We are following the route of the old embankment at this point until, at the far end of the hedge, pass through a gateway to the right, into the next field and then, a few yards ahead on the right, a stile of a sort gives access onto a surfaced path.

4 Now turn left along the modern embankment and note the remnants of its predecessor on the left. Here is a good point to survey the surroundings. The Lancashire fells and Pilling Church should be seen easily with the naked eye but by looking right, roughly in the direction of the embankment, the white buildings of Lancaster's university may be picked out near to the base of the hills. A little to the left of the university and perched on a hill is the Ashton Memorial. Heysham Power Station should be seen across Morecambe Bay while, over to the left, are

the Lake District mountains, including some of the highest such as Scafell Pike. The vista continues further to the left where Barrow shipyard can be discerned. When the atmospheric conditions are right it is even possible to see the Isle of Man, to the left of Barrow. Indeed, on a calm clear day this section of the walk can be a joy but in stormy conditions the going can be wretched as the wind-blown trees in the fields to the left will bear evidence. Fleetwood lies straight ahead, the Pharos Lighthouse standing prominent. Soon we approach the houses on Pilling Lane and eventually the caravan park, noted earlier. Further on, we reach the first houses of Knott End and, on reaching a slipway, continue along the shore until we meet the Esplanade where a plaque will be seen indicating the direction of various hills, mountains and other points of interest. Now follow the promenade towards the Bourne Arms, named after the Bourne family who owned much of the lands in the area from the sixteenth century. A little further is the Knott End Cafe. Turn left just before the cafe to reach the car park. Beyond the cafe are the toilets.

5 Turn right beyond Hackensall Hall, as directed by the Wyre Way sign to Barnabys Sands. The path soon re-enters the golf course where, once again, caution should be exercised; particular vigilance is required when crossing the fairway before the copse ahead on the right. Continue through to the far end of the course where our track swings to the right and on to a crossing of paths. The route ahead is to Barnaby's Sands whereas the path that cuts across was once the trackbed of a mineral branch line serving Preesall Salt Mines until its closure in the 1920s. To the right it led to a jetty on the Wyre but we now follow its path left as far as a junction of paths. Turn left here towards a farm and briefly enter the yard of Coat Walls Farm before turning immediately right and out again. Preesall and its windmill lie ahead. The path takes a left-hand corner and then a right-hand corner until, on reaching a T-junction, we turn right towards the Town Foot area of the village. From the 1890s progressive subsidence caused lakes to form but the most serious incident occurred in 1923 when a salt mine flooded and collapsed, causing surrounding land to disappear into the void and a farm to be demolished. On reaching the road junction turn left and walk up the road to the centre of Preesall.

6 At the junction in the centre of the village turn left to pass the Saracens Head and, a little further, the Black Bull on the left. It was at the Black Bull where in 1872 samples of rock were analysed leading to the discovery of salt. The road soon runs downhill to a bridge spanning the trackbed of the former branch line from Garstang to Knott End. On the right stood Preesall's single-platform station which closed to passengers from 1930 and to freight from 1950. Immediately over the bridge we need to turn left down the steps to a footpath – the trackbed of the old railway. In time we pass the rear of the farm at Curwens Hill on the left while, on the right, stands Parrox Hall in woodland. On reaching a junction of paths continue ahead into the woodland before emerging, in time, onto a residential road where we turn right and part company with the former trackbed. Now proceed to the end of the road to a junction in the small town centre. Turn left through the shopping area to the slipway and left again into the car park to return to the starting point.

WALK 23

Pilling Marsh

A walk through the interesting and historic village of Pilling to the marsh, from where there are excellent views towards the Lake District and the Lancashire fells. Choose a clear day and, if you have binoculars, take them!

Distance:	4¼ miles
Start:	The car park, diagonally opposite Pilling Pottery in the centre of the village. Grid reference: 403482
Map:	OS Pathfinders 658 and 668; OS Landranger 102
Time allowed:	No more than two hours (please note that the embankment is closed between 26th December and Good Friday each year to avoid disturbing over-wintering birds and sheep during the lambing season)
Conditions and difficulties:	Walking boots will be sufficient for most circumstances but, in dry spells, normal shoes may be worn. It is advisable to bring extra clothing as it can feel chilly by the estuary when there is a light wind
Facilities:	There are public toilets at the car park, a public house, shops and a payphone in the village centre
Public transport:	Pilling is served by a regular bus service from Fleetwood and Lancaster

1 Turn left from the car park along School Lane which, almost immediately, becomes Smallwood Hey. Following the road round the corner we soon reach a junction with Carr Lane on the left and the Methodist Church beyond. Just before the junction note the old cottage at the far end of a drive on the right. On the left, a little further on, is Smallwood Hey Farm House, a thatched farmhouse of some antiquity, and also on the same side, the Thatched House. These are isolated examples of older housing types surrounded mainly by houses of the twentieth century. Smallwood Hey is part of the old road to Preesall completed in about 1780, thus providing a safer and more reliable route than the shore road, which was often affected by the tides.

At the next crossroads turn right into Wheel Lane, signposted to the Shore. At a public footpath sign along this quiet lane the spire of the parish church can be seen across the fields to the right. The church spire is in fact a landmark for miles around and can be seen from the Lancashire fells. A hotel and restaurant are passed further along on the right before reaching Duck Street on the left. Eventually the road rises to a hump of a few feet in height. This was the first embankment to act as a sea defence and continued in that role until a new embankment was completed in 1983 at the edge of the shore. Subject to the restrictions mentioned above under 'Time allowed' turn left at the T-junction into Fluke Hall Lane and, after a short distance, a public footpath sign will be seen

Walk 23: Pilling Marsh

on the right, just beyond a driveway on the left, directing us to the coastal embankment via a track through a field. Now follow the directions under 2 below but if undertaking this walk during the restricted period turn right at Fluke Hall Lane and continue with the old embankment on the right. Although the views from this road are limited there are opportunities to survey the birdlife in the adjoining fields. Birds that are likely to be seen in winter include mallards, curlews, lapwing, redshank, pink-footed geese, oystercatchers, shelduck and partridges. Before long the road curves round towards the village once again and, just beyond the Golden Ball, at the junction with School Lane, turn right and follow the instructions under 4 below.

2 On reaching the embankment follow the path up the slope to the right for extensive views on a clear day across Morecambe Bay towards Barrow and the Lake District. Looking further to the right, below the Lancashire fells, the white line of buildings that comprise Lancaster University can also be seen. Continuing along the embankment we eventually cross Broad Fleet, as Pilling Water is known on its final stretch from Broadfleet Bridge to the sea. The path now begins to curve gently round to the left with the bay as we approach the Lane Ends amenity area. This is reached via a stile to the right of a gate. There are lakes fringed with trees below us to the right before reaching a car parking area. Follow the paved road through the car park to a gate by the side of a cattle grid and out onto a lane.

3 Turn right along the road (there is no pavement) and keep an eye out for the waders, ducks and geese that feed in the adjoining fields. In a little over half a mile we reach a junction just short of Broadfleet Bridge. Our route takes us across

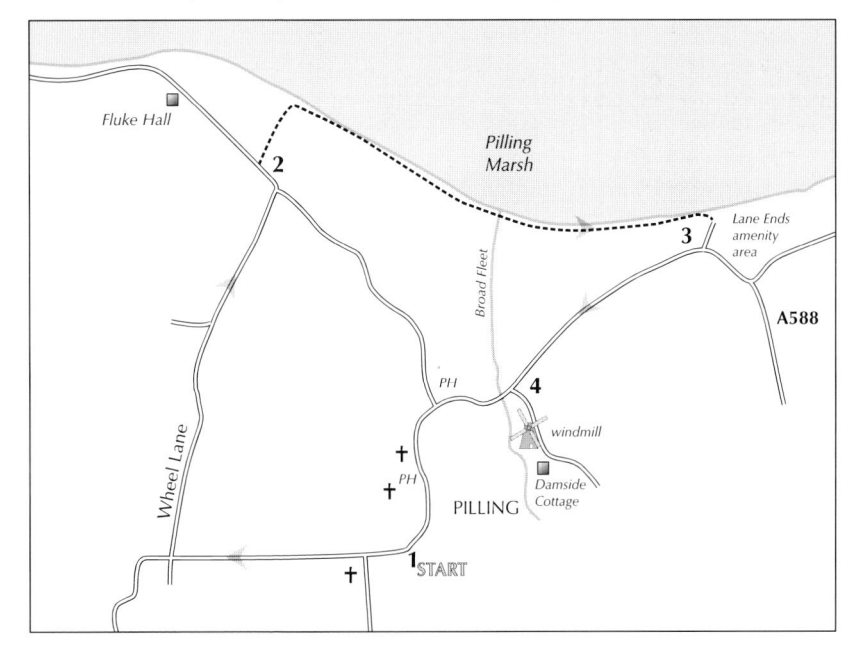

Pilling Church

the bridge but, first of all, it is worth a short diversion to the left to look at Damside Mill, one of only two surviving tower mills on the north side of the Wyre. It was built in 1808 by Ralph Slater, who was responsible for several mills on the Fylde, and is a six-storey example. It was converted to steam power from about 1885 and continued working until 1926. Since then it has found use as a private residence albeit without its sails. A little further along there is Damside Cottage, thought to have been the miller's house once. With a probable building date of late sixteenth or early seventeenth century, it could be one of the oldest houses in the area. The name 'Damside', incidentally, refers to a dam on Pilling Water.

4 Returning now to the junction, turn left across the bridge, which replaced a wooden seventeenth-century predecessor, and follow the road into the village. We pass the Golden Globe inn on the right before encountering the parish church of St John the Baptist. Its recessed spire is one of the most prominent features on this flat landscape making the church more familiar to people than its shy

– 104 –

Walk 23: Pilling Marsh

predecessor, a Georgian chapel of the same name, consecrated in 1721. It is, of course, most unusual for succeeding churches to survive virtually side by side but that is the case in Pilling. The older church became too small for its congregation and was replaced in 1887 but still survives as one of the finest examples of an unrestored Georgian church. Apart from its architectural merits it also has an association with a former incumbent, the Reverend George Holden, who devised tide estimation tables that are used to this day as the basis of tide calculations. There is a sundial over the main entrance in memory of this eighteenth-century curate. Access to the older church is not obvious but there is a track just beyond the Olde Ship inn on the right. Before reaching this old public house note the cheese press displayed outside and, almost opposite, the footpath signposted to the pinfold (a compound for stray animals). It is now a short distance back to our starting point, passing Pilling Pottery on the way.

The village of today, with its mixture of farms and houses, presents an image of continuity over a few centuries but, unlike the old Pilling, it has reasonable connections now with the outside world. The name is of Celtic derivation meaning 'small creek'. As a Celtic settlement it probably survived incursions from successive invaders due to the inhospitable surroundings but its isolated position, while offering a measure of inbuilt protection, made it difficult to benefit from links with the larger market centres such as Garstang and Lancaster. This may have been the reason why Pilling was not mentioned in the Domesday Book. The sea and the marshy hinterland effectively isolated the village until the reclaiming of the moss and subsequent road improvements.

WALK 24

Brock Valley and Bleasdale

Away from it all! Experience local fells and rivers that are bound closely to each other.

Distance:	9 miles
Start:	Follow signs from the A6 trunk road at Brock for Beacon Fell Country Park and then Chipping and Bleasdale until reaching Brock Mill Lane. Turn right to Brock Valley Nature Trail and start from the car park at the bottom of the hill, just before the bridge. Grid reference: 549431
Map:	OS Pathfinder 668; OS Landranger 102
Time allowed:	4½ hours
Conditions and difficulties:	Walking boots are likely to be suffficient in most conditions though some areas can become a little boggy. For those who are not supple some difficulty may be encountered in the woodlands near Jack Anderton Bridge
Facilities:	Come prepared as there are no local facilities available
Public transport:	Impractical for this walk

1 From the car park cross the bridge over the Brock. Turn left to enter the driveway to Brock Cottage Farm. Use the gap stile by the gateposts to turn left along a track but note the name on the gate across the track denoting Brock Mill. The name is a reminder that once there were mills in this valley powered by the waters of the Brock. The track ends at a stile just beyond some buildings on the right. Now enter a field and, a few yards in, turn right with the fence. Continue in this direction until drawing alongside the river on the left and follow it to reach a stile on the left that leads us on to a narrow path, fenced off from the adjoining field. Note how the river has cut into the steep bend on the opposite side, causing collapses of the ground above, bringing down trees at the top of the cliff from time to time. Eventually the path parts company with the river to enter the woods. We climb through the trees to emerge above the woods and reach a junction of tracks. Turn left here and follow the track above the river noting the aqueduct carrying water pipes. The track now drops down towards an old building bearing the inscription WW1721. Before reaching the building, however, turn right into the woods just at the point where the track bends to the left to pass the building. Entering the woods, follow the narrow path to the left and continue along the bottom edge of the woodland with a field on the left. Eventually the path returns to the riverside and, where it does, another path joins us on the left. The path can be a little muddy in parts even in fairly dry times, owing to moisture from above, but it becomes broader as the woodland thins out on the approach to a bridge across the Brock. Here there are two paths rising on our right. Take the first of these, a sunken lane with a secondary track on its right.

Walk 24: Brock Valley and Bleasdale

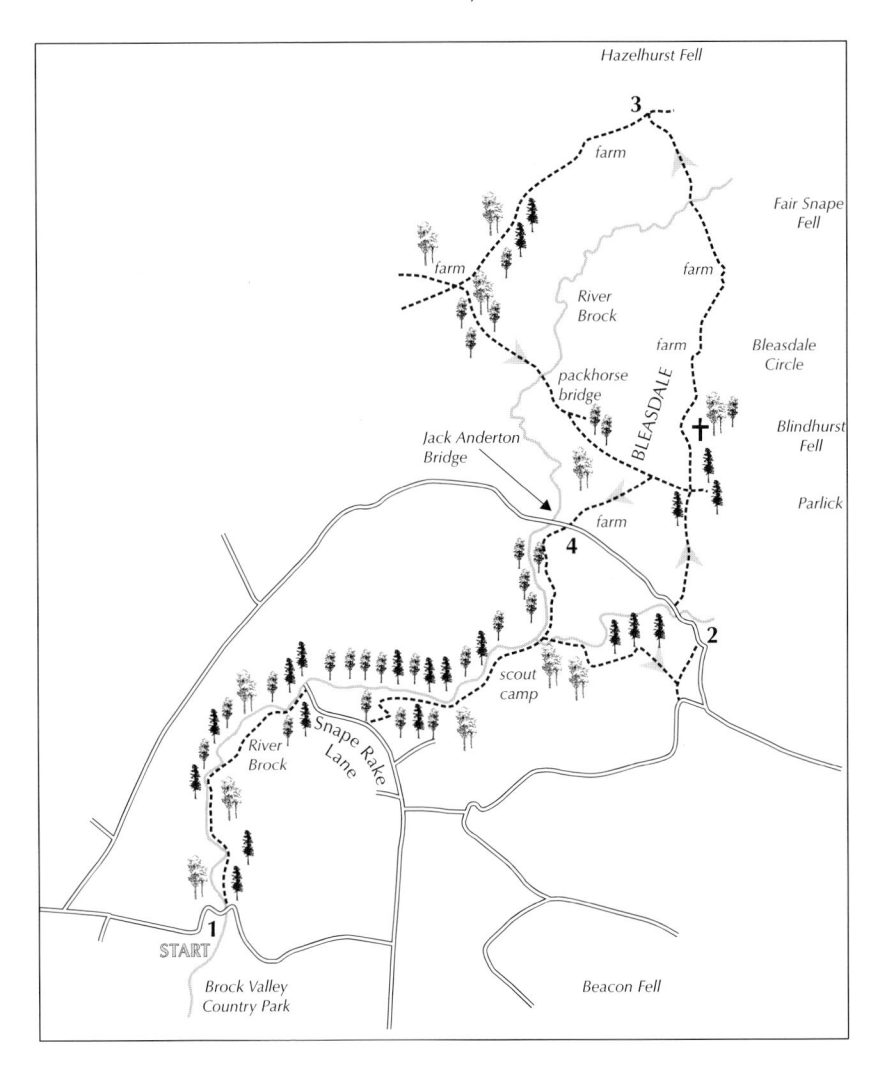

This is Snape Rake Lane, of Roman origin, and is moist for much of its steep ascent through the woods. On reaching the top edge of the woods we transfer to a tarmac road and continue along a straight and fairly level stretch. The road then rises and levels up again as Beacon Fell comes into view on the right. Just as the road is about to bend to the right note some gateposts and a gate just inside the wood on the left. Take the path around the gate and follow it as it drops down and round a hairpin bend until reaching the valley floor. It is important to note our position because, when we retrace our steps, the steep path may be overlooked. There is a sign at the bottom indicating a bridleway to the right but, if this is missed, don't worry; just turn right and follow the river until reaching an open grassy clearing used by the Waddecar Scout Camp for various activities. Resume alongside the river and, after a while, the path swings round to the left

Fylde Coast and Country Walks

Left: Snape Rake Lane

Below: Tributary of the Brock near Admarsh Barn Farm

Walk 24: Brock Valley and Bleasdale

into another clearing and, ahead, one can see the solid shape of Fair Snape Fell, identified by the cairn on top. At the far end of the clearing a pair of stiles will be seen ahead in a fence. They lead us into a field from where we continue in the same direction until, at the far side of the field, a gateway will be seen in the fence ahead. Pass through into another field, along its left-hand side until reaching a footbridge close to where the river splits.

We shall return via the bridge but, for now, we must turn right without crossing the river, passing the mossy ruins of an old barn to reach a stile above the river. Follow the narrow path through the woods to eventually reach a footbridge across a stream. Keep on the rising path until reaching a stile at the upper edge of the valley, leading us into a field with the conical shape of Parlick looming up ahead. This is one of the fells on whose slopes the water gathers to form the streams that eventually merge as the river Brock so there is a strong bond between river and hill. Aim directly for Parlick across the tussocky field, keeping a little to the left of Parlick to locate a stile to the left of a gate and continue along the left-hand edge of the next field towards the farm ahead. The wooded Beacon Fell is clearly visible on the right as we reach a stile by a gateway on our left towards the far end of the field. Once over the stile we change direction and head directly for the fells. Soon the road to Bleasdale Church will be seen between the fields below. Continuing along the right-hand edge of the field we drop down to a stile in the far right-hand corner and take the steps down to the road.

2 Turn left and follow the lane down to pass Smithy Cottage which, as the name suggests, was once the blacksmith's forge. More recently it was a post office and store providing a welcome outpost, not only for walkers and cyclists but for locals who, since its closure, have a journey of several miles to the nearest shop. Indeed, there is hardly any shop left between Chipping and the M6! Continue along the lane just a short way and take the first turning on the right (the road seen earlier from the field above) leading to Bleasdale Church. The road rises initially and then proceeds between unfenced fields. At a junction take the left fork, passing woodland on the left, to reach a school and then, further on, St Eadmer's Church of Admarsh-in-Bleasdale, its exterior coat of roughcast intended to protect the fabric of the building from the worst of the weather. Believed to date from the reign of Elizabeth I it was rebuilt in the nineteenth century.

Now go on over the cattle grid and, beyond a crest in the road at a gentle left-hand bend, Vicarage Farm appears ahead, below Hazelhurst Fell. Beyond the field on our right is a woodland where a Bronze Age circle was discovered in 1898. It was a circular village site of the period surrounded by a ditch and remnants of the discovery are preserved at the Harris Museum in Preston. Just as we approach the farm the road bends to the right, over a cattle grid and through a small woodland. Opposite the rear entrance to the farm on the left is a concessionary path on the right to Bleasdale Circle. Beyond the next cattle grid we return to the open. Looking up to the right we can see the grooves in the side of Parlick, worn by the hill streams that come together to form the river Brock.

The buildings ahead are Admarsh Barn Farm and to the left of these, and behind, is the substantial house known as Hazelhurst. The road curves round to enter the farm but immediately beyond the gates turn right through a small pedestrian gate to follow the boundary fence along a grassy path around the outside of the

Parlick from Bleasdale

buildings, through a second small gate and on to a stile at the far end of the farm. Now continue along the right-hand edge of a field to join a track which leads down to a low stone bridge over one of the tributaries of the Brock that flows from Fair Snape Fell. Here we see the Brock as a moorland stream in contrast to the broader river of the woodlands and the slower and deeper river it has become by the time it joins the Wyre at St Michael's. Onwards through the next gate we soon reach two footbridges across a major tributary. This is a delightful spot and an ideal place to take in the views. Beyond the footbridge a stile to the left of a gate leads us into the next field where we continue along the right-hand edge until the brook on the right veers away. Then aim for the centre of the fence at the far side of the field where a stile will be found between the hawthorn trees. From here rise half-left through a rough, tussocky field towards the small woodland up on the left and then continue until reaching the track beyond.

3. We are now at the foot of Hazelhurst Fell and must now turn left along the track, passing in between the buildings at Hazelhurst. There was once a hamlet situated here known as Coolan, where a small cottage industry was carried on but there are very few remains now. Beyond the buildings we cross a cattle grid by the entrance to the cobbled farmyard and follow the rising gradient to emerge into the open again. On a clear day there are extensive views from here. At a crest the road bends to the left and the fells once again open themselves up to our gaze before the road falls gently to cross a cattle grid and enter a wood.

Now proceed along a made-up road (of stone flags rather than tarmac) that eventually drops down to a bridge over Clough Heads Brook reaching us courtesy of the steep slopes of Hazelhurst Fell. From here we rise again for the first time in a while to reach a group of buildings at Brooks Barn, a working farm. At a T-junction with a gate opposite turn left to return into woodland. At the far end we emerge into the open again and, at a junction, take the left fork that leads

Walk 24: Brock Valley and Bleasdale

to Brooks Farm. On passing the farm and its cobbled courtyard we reach a bridge across a tributary that we crossed earlier, north of Admarsh Barn Farm. Across to our left is an old packhorse bridge and one can only hope that the incline to the right of it was less severe than it appears to be now! Now rising with the road we are soon joined by a beech hedge on our left. Ignore a track on the left as we return to woodland, catching another brief view of the encircling fells before we do. Beyond the woodland there is a view of Bleasdale Church before the road becomes enclosed by beech hedges.

Look out for a gate in the hedge on the right, about 50 yards before a left-hand bend, and then aim half-right towards a small barn (to the right of a house ahead). Continue to the barn, ignoring stiles on the way, and a track develops in the field leading directly to a gate. Continue along the stony track into the centre of the farmyard and then follow the right of way to the left of the farmhouse and out onto a road.

4 Turn right but then almost immediately left and up onto an embankment, close to Jack Anderton Bridge, and follow the path along the edge of the wood, ignoring a stile on the left. Looking down to the river one can see the Jack Anderton Bridge carrying the road over the Brock. There is a narrow ledge overlooking the wooded valley below and one or two other sections may be a little tricky in wet conditions but otherwise the path maintains an attractive course at the top edge of the wood before reaching a stile in a fence ahead. From here drop down towards the river, finding a course in between the gorse bushes to emerge into a field. At the far end of this field is the footbridge we encountered earlier that takes us over the main tributary of the Brock. Beyond the bridge we retrace our steps, following the river downstream for the time being. Passing through fields we reach the double stile at the entrance to the Waddecar Scout Camp Adventure Area. Follow the broad track until, drawing close to the small toilet block on the left, turn right through the grassy clearing and keep the river in sight as we return into woodland. Keep a careful look out for a post pointing a change of direction to the left to follow a path up the bank. The path is indistinct at first but the line of the path should be seen as it rises before it almost double backs on itself at a hairpin bend and up to a gate leading to Snape Rake Lane.

Turn right down this lane but take care as the tarmac surface gives way to a mixture of stone, earth and water as it descends steeply to a ford over the river. Don't cross the bridge but turn left at this point to follow the Brock downstream. Continue alongside the field at the bottom edge of the wood until the path joins a track just beyond a solitary building. Turn left up the track, passing the large pipes on the right that cross the Brock. At a point about 30 yards before reaching a gate across the track follow a vague path over the banking on the right and down into the trees via a series of steps to reach the river once again. Now follow the clearly defined path between the river and the fields until we eventually reach a stile leading into a field. Turn right and keep by the fence until it bends round to the right. From here veer a little to the left and, further on, follow the left-hand boundary fence as we approach a group of buildings. Continue over a stile and along a track, passing buildings until reaching the drive to Brock Cottage Farm. Once through the gap stile, turn right over the bridge and left into the car park.

WALK 25

Whitechapel and Beacon Fell

Shake off the cobwebs with this invigorating walk up to Beacon Fell. Remember to choose a clear day when the views from the fell should be all the more rewarding.

Distance:	3½ miles
Start:	Initially follow signs for Beacon Fell from Broughton and then for Inglewhite and Whitechapel. Park near the school and the entrance to the village hall. Grid reference: 557415
Map:	OS Pathfinder 668; OS Landranger 102
Time allowed:	2¼ hours
Conditions and difficulties:	Walking boots are likely to be sufficient except after rainy spells when Wellington boots may be preferable
Facilities:	There is a visitor centre, including toilets, on Beacon Fell and it is advisable to bring binoculars to scan the extensive views from the fell. There is the unusual Cross Keys Inn that is part of a working farm and a public telephone box near the starting point
Public transport:	There is a very limited bus service

1 From our parking spot near to the school, walk the few yards towards the left-hand bend and turn right over a stile and into a small field. Proceed, parallel to the hedge on our left, to the far side where a further stile is negotiated. Keep to the left side of the next field. Beacon Fell is prominent on the right while, behind and further on, stands Hazelhurst Fell. As we breast the slight brow veer a little to the right to reach a footbridge with a stile. Now continue in the same direction through a field, between trees that mark a former boundary, and aim for the middle of a group of buildings ahead. An access drive separates these buildings and a gate is our exit point from the field to the drive, along which we proceed to reach a road.

Turn right, passing the brightly patterned black-and-white Eccles Moss Cottage and Eccles Moss Farm but, when level with the farm, look out for a public footpath sign on the left. Turn here and take the stile to pass between the trees. Look out for a stile in the fence on the right towards the far end of the trees. Once over this stile head across the field keeping to the left of the white cottage below the wooded Beacon Fell. Once over the brow a gate will be seen in a fence. As we pass through the gate we need to aim a little to the left for the farm buildings. Another gate by a stream will be seen at the far side of the field. From here we must head left to a third gate from which we follow a track round to the right where it straightens between trees to give the appearance of an avenue. At a farm take a stile to the right of a gate and enter the farmyard. Proceed in a straight line ahead through gates as we pass White Lee Farm with White Lee Hall on the left. A driveway then leads us to a road. White Lee Farm

– 112 –

Walk 25: Whitechapel and Beacon Fell

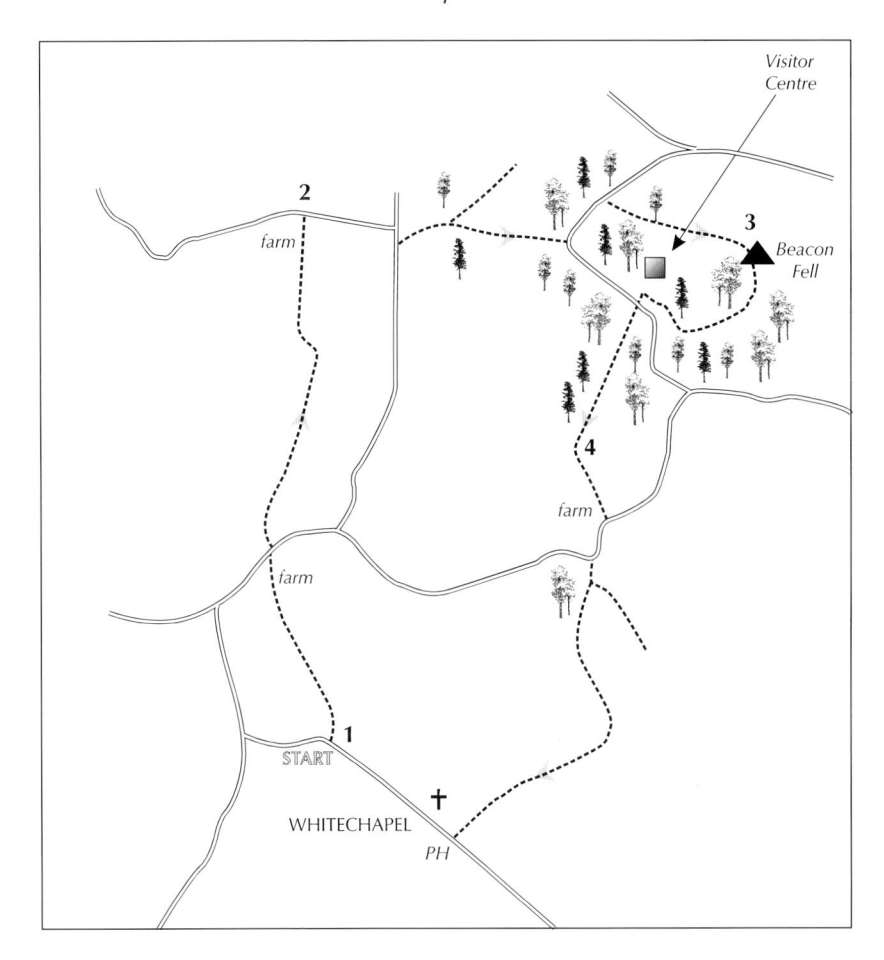

was once owned by the Kighley family, one of whom joined the Jacobite Rebellion of 1715 but was later forced to flee the country.

2 Turn right, up White Lee Lane, tree-lined with an unusually broad grassy bank on the left, to reach a T-junction. Turn right along Bleasdale Road for just a few yards and then look for a stile on the bank to the left, before the brow of the road. From the stile head away from the road towards the foot of the fell. This is where the serious work begins. A footbridge will be seen at the far side of the field in between small plantations of trees. From the footbridge a grassy path veers to the left but we must keep straight ahead, upwards to a slatted stile in a fence. It is worth looking back at this point because, although we have only climbed a few metres, the view has quickly opened up to take in the Fylde and the mosslands north of the Wyre. Continue up the steep slope to the conifer plantation above but aim for the top corner of the field to locate a stone step stile that leads us into another field below a much larger plantation. From the stone stile there is a commanding view over west Lancashire; indeed, whereas

many of the other walks allow us to look at parts of the Fylde in detail we now have the opportunity of taking an overview, relating the various natural and man-made features to each other. Preston and its landmarks can also be seen with the naked eye: the slender spire of St Walburge, the mills and the tall offices of the city centre. On a clear day it is possible to see the Lake District mountains and Barrow in the north, the Welsh hills and Liverpool's Anglican Cathedral (with binoculars) in the south and even the Isle of Man, nearly eighty miles to the west. With good local knowledge, of course, much more can be identified. Resuming the climb up the fell we cover the short distance to the next stile and into a plantation but, almost immediately, we reach a road.

At the road turn left and follow it for a short distance round to the right. We need to look out for a gap between plantations on the right, beyond a dry stone boundary wall but before reaching a small lay-by on the left. Through the gap we need to follow the rather indistinct path which becomes more established as we climb up past the large plantation on our right. Soon we cross another path and, immediately, the curvaceous slopes of Parlick appear ahead. Further up, another path is encountered before we climb the final section to the summit of Beacon Fell marked by a white triangulation point at 873 feet high (or 266 metres). The name of this fell comes from the fire beacon that was used since Roman times, partly to guide travellers through difficult terrain but also to warn of danger or some important event. It is easy to see how warning signals could be transmitted considerable distances in a short time.

3 Having arrived at the summit remember to turn right after taking in the views of the higher fells to the east. Our way down is along a well established path that

Beacon Fell

Walk 25: Whitechapel and Beacon Fell

soon crosses another path before changing direction to the right. As the path meets a further path by some picnic tables turn right and now head towards the car park and visitor centre.

From the visitor centre and its car park cross the road to a lower car park and aim for the left-hand corner to follow a footpath that soon splits in two. Take the right fork to pass through trees, pursuing a fairly straight course to a stile in a fence at the bottom of the plantation. Good views are available to the west once again.

4 From the stile go forward until farm buildings become visible to our left and then aim for a stile next to a gate in a fence to the left. From here head directly towards the farm buildings and, as we do so, note the gradually rising ridge of the aptly named Longridge Fell in the middle distance, to the left of the buildings. As we approach the farm the field narrows to reach a gate between farm buildings (ignore the gate in a wall on the left). A stile to the right of the gate leads into the farmyard and we pass straight through to reach a lane on a bend. Before leaving the farm it is worth recalling that a former occupier, Richard Cromblesholme, was convicted in 1574 as a papist and imprisoned in the Tower of London.

Turn right and follow the road to a right-hand bend where we turn left to cross a stile by a gate. Follow the track through a wooded area and cross a stream where there is a small waterfall on the right, hidden from the road. The track now splits in two and we curve round to the right into a field. Where the track peters out look diagonally left towards Whitechapel, identified by a group of white buildings and, to the left of them, a chapel. We need to turn left across the field so that we are walking parallel to a stand of trees that lie to the left of the village. As we cross the field below a brow, the right-hand boundary should be seen below. Keep on through this long field, still maintaining a parallel course to the trees on our right, until eventually approaching the far corner. Drop down to the right-hand boundary to locate a stile before the corner. This leads us into a small enclosed field and to another stile, a few yards further on. From this stile we need to strike a course half-left, roughly between the left-hand and right-hand edges of the field, through a line of trees to reach a gate. From here continue a little to the right where a gate will be seen beyond a stream. Ignore the stile on the right but pass through the gate and follow the track to another gate onto the road through Whitechapel.

Opposite is the Cross Keys Inn, unusual in that it is also part of a working farm. Turn right to pass St James's Church with a bellcote. Believed to date from the eighteenth century it replaced an earlier chapel built for the Threlfalls of Ashes Farm, situated south east of Whitechapel. The village once supported a small domestic weaving industry but, though the handloom weavers have long since disappeared, the weavers' cottages survive. It is now a short distance to Whitechapel County Primary School and our starting point.

WALK 26

Inglewhite

A very pleasant walk delving deep into the heart of the Lancashire countryside.

Distance:	5½ miles
Start:	Initially follow signs for Beacon Fell from Broughton and then for Inglewhite. From the large lay-by, opposite the small church and south of the Green Man public house in the centre of the village. Grid reference: 547398
Map:	OS Pathfinder 679; OS Landranger 102
Time allowed:	3 hours
Conditions and difficulties:	Walking boots are likely to be sufficient in dry conditions but, after prolonged periods of rain and during winter months it can be muddy in parts and Wellington boots may be preferred
Facilities:	The Green Man public house in Inglewhite and the adjoining public telephone box
Public transport:	There is a very limited bus service

1 From the lay-by walk away from the village as far as a house that is set back on the left. The right of way is up the drive and then to the right, in front of the house, before working our way to the back, between the house and the car ports and then curving round to the left to locate a stile in a hedge. Cross over the stile and keep along the right-hand side of the field to where it turns right. Follow the boundary to the right, through a gate and then left with the hedge in the next field to a gap stile. Carry on over a stream from where the right of way is directly ahead to a gate at the top of the field. At the time of writing a barbed wire fence stands in the way but there is a stile at the right-hand end of this fence. Therefore I suggest that, after the stile is negotiated, return along the other side of the fence and then follow the correct right of way, up the field to locate the gate in the roadside hedge about twenty yards in from the corner.

Turn right but, before reaching the first house, turn right again along a bridleway. Initially, it is an access road to houses but where it swings round to a private house continue ahead along the track that curves to the right and drops down to a gate. Beyond the gate is a ford with a footbridge to the side – a picturesque spot. Climbing up the track on the other side we reach a gate at a farm. Continue ahead between the barn and the house to pass through another gate and onwards to a lane.

Turn right and then first left into Curwen Lane. On a clear day Winter Hill, with its television mast, should be visible ahead in the distance. Where the lane makes a left turn at a corner we need to turn right at a gate and proceed along the left-hand edge of the field, passing power cables as we do so. A small wood with a pool is encountered on the left as we continue over a footbridge and along the left-hand edge of the next field. At a stile in the far left-hand corner

Walk 26: Inglewhite

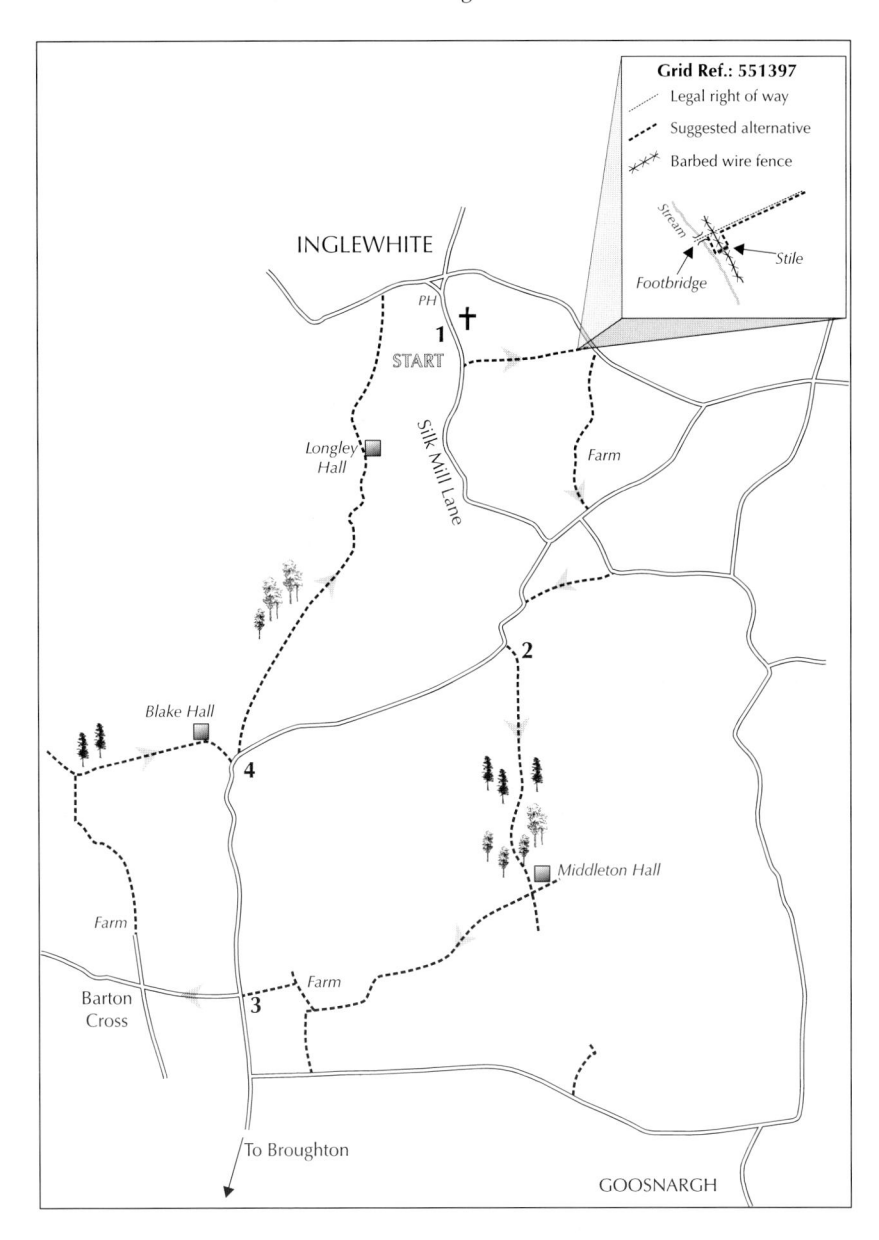

we emerge onto a road and turn left, taking care as we proceed around a left-hand bend to a sharp right-hand corner.

2. At this point take the bridleway on the left along a private road, passing the Gate House on the right and the well-proportioned Goosnargh Lodge on the left with a splendid Cedar of Lebanon tree behind the house. The access road ends at the

last house on the right but we continue in the same direction onto a grassy track. We pass through a wooded area before the track drops down to the meandering Westfield Brook which can be crossed by a footbridge beside a ford. This is another pleasant spot where the wide brook has eaten away at a field edge to form a steep cutting. We now need to climb up the other side before the track drops down, through gates, to a junction of tracks. Less than a mile ahead lies Goosnargh but we must now take the stile in front of us and left of the second of two gates on the right.

From the stile proceed along the right-hand edge of the field to reach a pond on the right. Now head half-left, over the brow of the field, to locate a stile in a hedge on the right-hand side. Cross the stile and head directly away towards farm buildings while keeping to the left-hand edge. Near to the far left-hand corner a stile will be found in the hedge. Cross over and continue across a small field to a footbridge. Don't cross the bridge, though, but take the track to the right through a gateway and into an adjoining field. Now head left to the far left-hand corner. Pass through a gate and carry on along a track to the main farm access road at a T-junction. Don't turn right into the farmyard but, instead, pass through the gate ahead and walk round the slurry storage tank in the field corner to follow the right-hand edge of the field. There are farm buildings on our right but, shortly beyond the last of the buildings, turn left to cross the field towards the road on the far side just at the point where a house stands at a junction of roads. A stile will be seen near a field corner, to the left of the house ahead.

3 From the stile cross the road straight into Barton Lane, less than a mile from the M6 motorway. Ahead of us stands Barton church spire as we continue along the lane to Barton Cross, re-erected in 1901 on the same stone block as the old cross. In the Middle Ages many such wayside crosses were erected at various places on the way to the church so that the coffin bearers could rest the coffin and pray. The cross stands at the end of a lane, opposite the access road to Cross Farm on the right. It is to the right that we must now turn, directly to the farmyard, through which we pass, keeping to the right of the buildings in the centre to locate large gates ahead. Take the stile in the paddock ahead and aim for the far left-hand edge where a further stile provides access onto a broad track between fences. Turn right and continue to two gates. The track drops down to a ford via the right-hand gate but we must take the stile by the left-hand gate to drop down the field a short way before turning left towards a footbridge on the far boundary. Cross the bridge and turn half-right up the next field to a brow. Beyond the brow look down to the left towards another footbridge. A stile to the right of this bridge gives us access into the next field. From here turn right, keeping quite close to the right-hand boundary, climbing a bank above the brook on the left. Ignore a stile on the right but look out for buildings ahead. Keep on towards them and cross a footbridge and stile into another field. Remaining with the left-hand boundary we soon reach Blake Hall. Aim for the left-hand corner, left of a barn, and locate a stile by a gate. Turn right and up the access road to reach a lane on a sharp bend.

4 Turn left just a few yards and look for a stile up the bank on the left that takes us into a field. Now head half-right and drop down to a stile, from where we

Walk 26: Inglewhite

The market cross at Inglewhite

veer a little to the right, rising again to a brow. Now we need to aim for the right-hand edge of the long stretch of woodland ahead where a stile will be found at the far side of the field. Continue with the woodland on our left. The conical shape of Parlick can be seen ahead as we keep going in the same direction to reach a gate in the far boundary (ignore the gate further down by the stream). Now go forward to a footbridge over Sparling Brook from where there is a choice of paths. Keep along the track that veers up and round to the left. At the top of the field the track passes through a gateway but we must turn right before the gateway, alongside a hedge until, just before reaching a pond, turn left over a stile and along an enclosed track leading directly to Longley Hall. Pass in between the buildings to the access track on the far side. This leads us unerringly to Bilsborrow Lane where we turn right to cover the short distance back to Inglewhite. Turn right by the market cross but, before doing so, it is worth a look around the green where there is an attractive composition of houses (the oldest of seventeenth-century origin) and farms. Although the village may appear to be a haven of tranquillity now it is worth contemplating how busy it must have been when the nationally-known annual cattle fair was held here. The market cross is dated 1675 but part of it is believed to date from a much earlier time. It was restored by public subscription in 1911. Now turn right past the Green Man along Silk Mill Lane, a reminder of the former silk mill situated close to the brook, and back to the lay-by, opposite Inglewhite Congregational Church.